The Glory Of Our Weakness

Sermons
With Children's Lessons
For Lent And Easter

Erskine White

CSS Publishing Company, Inc., Lima, Ohio

THE GLORY OF OUR WEAKNESS

Copyright © 1997 by
CSS Publishing Company, Inc.
Lima, Ohio

All rights reserved. No part of this publication may be reproduced in any manner whatsoever without the prior permission of the publisher, except in the case of brief quotations embodied in critical articles and reviews. Inquiries should be addressed to: Permissions, CSS Publishing Company, Inc., P.O. Box 4503, Lima, Ohio 45802-4503.

Scripture quotations are from the *New Revised Standard Version of the Bible*, copyright 1989 by the Division of Christian Education of the National Council of the Churches of Christ in the USA. Used by permission.

Scripture quotations marked (NIV) are taken from the *Holy Bible, New International Version*. Copyright © 1973, 1978, 1984 International Bible Society. Used by permission of Zondervan Bible Publishers. All rights reserved.

Scripture quotations marked (RSV) are from the *Revised Standard Version of the Bible*, copyrighted 1945, 1952 ©, 1971, 1973, by the Division of Christian Education of the National Council of the Churches of Christ in the USA. Used by permission.

Library of Congress Cataloging-in-Publication Data

White, Erskine, 1951-
   The glory of our weakness : sermons for Lent and Easter / Erskine White.
     p.   cm.
   ISBN 0-7880-1135-9 (pbk.)
   1. Lenten sermons. 2. Easter—Sermons. 3. Children's sermons. 4. Sermons, American. I. Title.
BV4277.W54   1998
252'.62—dc21   97-27359
                                                                                            CIP

ISBN 0-7880-1135-9   PRINTED IN U.S.A.

This final book of sermons
is dedicated to my wife

Caroline Blackwell White

and to our children

Daniel Franklin White
Joshua Leeland White
Jordan Christa White

*

*It doesn't seem like a long, long time
Since we were born again
Into the dazzling light
Uniting black and white.
You are the rich brown earth;
I am the flowers that grow.*

*We'll have children of the kingdom;
They won't be torn by war,
Nor will they kill or hate
Or hesitate
To love justice.*

lyrics from "Ruby Jean & Billie Lee"
by Jim Seals and Dash Crofts
© 1973 Sutjujo Music and Faizilu Publishing (BMI)
Used with permission. All rights reserved.

Table Of Contents

INTRODUCTION — 9

ASH WEDNESDAY — 15
  Where The Spirit Must Live Or Die
  (Matthew 4:1-11)
  Pastoral Prayer

FIRST SUNDAY IN LENT — 23
  Giving Up For Lent
  (John 5:2-9)
  Pastoral Prayer
  Children's Lesson
    The Power Of Love

SECOND SUNDAY IN LENT — 33
  The Glory Of Our Weakness
  (Exodus 3:9-20; Romans 8:26-30)
  Pastoral Prayer
  Children's Lesson
    God's People Are The Little People

THIRD SUNDAY IN LENT — 45
  The Day God Changed His Mind
  (Jonah 3)
  Pastoral Prayer
  Children's Lesson
    The Things We Don't Want To Do

FOURTH SUNDAY IN LENT   55
    Christians Too Busy To Pray
    (Luke 22:39-46)
    Pastoral Prayer
    Children's Lesson
       Even Jesus Was Scared

FIFTH SUNDAY IN LENT   65
    Barabbas Speaks
    (Matthew 27:15-26)
    Pastoral Prayer
    Children's Lesson
       Jealous Of The Good

PALM SUNDAY/PASSION SUNDAY   75
    The Strength To See It Through
    (Isaiah 50:4-9a; Mark 11:1-10)
    Pastoral Prayer
    Children's Lesson
       From Victim To Victor

MAUNDY THURSDAY   85
    The Judas In Us All
    (John 13:21-30)

EASTER SUNDAY   89
    Resurrection Of The Heart
    (Jeremiah 31:31-34; Luke 24:36-49)
    Pastoral Prayer
    Children's Lesson
       Ghost Stories

SUNDAY AFTER EASTER   99
    Late For Easter
    (John 20:19-31)
    Pastoral Prayer
    Children's Lesson
       Be A Doubting Thomas

A Word About Language

The language in this book pertaining to people is inclusive of men and women. Similarly, the anecdotes and illustrations have been deliberately varied so as to include the experiences of women and men alike. As for the language pertaining to God, I have used pronouns (generally "He" for God and "She" for the Holy Spirit). It is necessary to use pronouns in order to preserve the biblical insistence that ours is a personal God. Whenever it appears, however, the pronoun is always capitalized, indicating to the reader that God is neither male nor female in human terms.

— E. White

Introduction

Over a century ago, in 1880, the great Russian writer Feodor Dostoevski published *The Brothers Karamazov*, a book many consider the most sublime Christian novel ever composed. Indeed, the Catholic critic Maurice Baring said of this book, "Supposing the Gospel of St. John were annihilated and lost to us forever; although nothing could replace it, Dostoevski's work would more nearly replace it than any other book written by any other man." Sigmund Freud, himself no friend of religion, nonetheless felt that "*The Brothers Karamazov* is the most magnificent novel ever written, and the story of the Grand Inquisitor is one of the peaks of the literature of the world. It can hardly be overpraised."

The story of the Grand Inquisitor appears as a story-within-a-story in the middle of Dostoevski's novel. In it, Jesus Christ comes back to earth, appearing in Spain at the height of the fearsome Inquisition. The common people, cowed by the terror of hooded heresy hunters and the dreaded *auto-da-fé*, instinctively recognize Christ and flock to Him in adoration and need, but the institutional church, as represented by the Grand Inquisitor, promptly puts Jesus in jail. The rest of Dostoevski's story consists of a dialogue between the Inquisitor and Christ, although it is a dialogue in which the latter never says a word.

Basically, the Grand Inquisitor explains to the presumably clueless Christ why the Church has become so different from the Nazarene whose name it bears. Jesus offers freedom, the Inquisitor declares, while the Church offers bread, and most people, if forced to choose, will choose bread. In other words, the Galilean's simple message of not worrying about tomorrow, of not acquiring worldly wealth but being filled with the riches of heaven, of loving one's enemies and not living or dying by the sword, of praying in secret and not acting like the "religious" folks who flaunt their piety before others — Jesus' message of placing radical, joyful trust in God for all the things we truly need is simply too hard for most people in the real world, the old Inquisitor opines. The way shown by Jesus Christ, the Word made flesh, demands far more than we children of flesh can give.

In effect, the Inquisitor tells his Prisoner, "You were cruel to come with teachings which are manifestly beyond the abilities of millions of human beings." By contrast, the Church is much more compassionate than Christ. By offering bread instead of freedom, the Church compromises the way of Christ to easier, more manageable terms, thereby placing the requirements and rewards of salvation within the grasp of the masses of ordinary seekers.

In Dostoevski's tale, the Inquisitor makes cogent arguments. Still, the reader senses that the Inquisitor remains uneasy, as if knowing somewhere within himself that the Prisoner to whom he speaks is unpersuaded. Somehow, despite Christ's silence and the Church's power to incarcerate Him, the Inquisitor knows that this Prisoner's opinion is still all-important. As for Jesus, His only reply when the Inquisitor concludes is to render His ecclesial jailer a silent kiss. Then, the story of the Grand Inquisitor ends with swift and magnificent simplicity: "The kiss glows in [the Inquisitor's] heart, but the old man adheres to his idea."

Dostoevski wrote a powerful parable indeed, but is he right? Is he right to say that contrary to the lofty mission statements we publish and proclaim, the Church's actual mission in the world is to water down the faith and spirit of Jesus Christ? Is the Church profiting and "succeeding" in worldly terms by making Jesus' "hard sayings" and revolutionary demands more accessible — by making the lifestyle of God's radical redemption more palatable to a militantly unredeemed world? And if so, so what? Given the limited capacity for transcendence which is the human condition, is this perhaps a necessary, even a good thing, for the Church to do?

Today as in every age, Christian preachers and parishioners alike embody within themselves and their communities the disturbing dialogue Dostoevski so masterfully put to paper. For example, the Church owns tremendous stores of property, power, and prestige; thus, by its own wealth and possessions, the Church stamps an ecclesiastical *imprimatur* on the material "good life" we idolize with such joyless frenzy in our secular, capitalist culture. The Church remains at the congregational level the most thoroughly segregated major institution in America; thus do Christian churches every Sunday legitimate (or at least fail to repudiate) the sinful divisions of income, race, and ideology which bedevil our nation and cause such offense to God.[1]

When taking political action in the public square today, churches, both liberal and conservative alike, are as liable, each in their own ways, to exhibit intolerance, arrogance, bigotry, and self-righteousness as love, humility, justice, and peace. Indeed, even within its own walls, the Christian Church is as susceptible as is any secular institution to vicious conflicts, partisan purges, ugly power plays, and unholy rages ... as too many pastors, former pastors, and other "wounded healers" know all too well.

There is a well-documented gap in American society today between "believing and belonging" — Americans believe in God and engage in spiritual journeys in record numbers, while real church participation flattens out in some denominations and declines in others. Media experts attribute this trend to the alleged inability of "baby boomers" to make commitments, the increased mobility of American families, and so on, but Dostoevski offers a far more transcendent and timeless answer. The gap which lies at the heart of the matter is the spirit of a Church which looks, acts, and believes more like the Grand Inquisitor than Jesus Christ.

What Dostoevski called the problem of offering bread over freedom, the great Nazi-era martyr Dietrich Bonhoeffer called "cheap grace." In Christ "there is neither Jew nor Greek, there is

---

1. It should be noted that the Church does outpace society in one area of integration. Religious congregations of all faiths generally have a much better mix of generations than do other major American institutions, such as schools, business, the military, or government. In an age of young family subdivisions and seniors-only condominium developments, this intermingling of the young and old in local churches is not insignificant. However, the Church does lag far behind schools, the workplace, the military, *et al* in terms of the other forms of segregation mentioned above.

neither slave nor free, there is neither male nor female" (Galatians 3:28), and to walk with Him is to "be not conformed to this world" (Romans 12:2). Yet in too many ways which sadden and dismay, the Church so conforms to the values and priorities of the world as to make it all too easy to "be a Christian" in the world. When this happens, Christianity, while popular and pervasive, becomes anemic and trivialized. Society suffers as well from the absence of a militant corporate witness to radical Christian love in its midst.

Yet always where the Christian Church is concerned, there is more to be said and affirmed. Always there is that indomitable Presence and beckoning Spirit which so unsettled the Inquisitor and attracted the multitudes. "The kiss [of Christ] glows in his heart," Dostoevski wrote. Or, in the post-Easter experience of Christ's apostles, *"Were not our hearts burning within us while he was talking to us?"* (Luke 24:32b). Always, there remains within the Church, in pulpit and pews, those whose hearts still burn as the living Christ moves and speaks among them. Even those who leave the Church still love Christ enough to carry that flame as well. Somehow, by the grace of God, Christ is never completely overwhelmed by Christianity, nor faith overcome by religion.

This book of sermons is offered for all those, both within and without the Church, who remain challenged and inspired by the call of Christ and the promise of Christian *koinonia*. However, this book is offered with special affection and admiration for preachers still laboring every week within the Church, in the pastor's study and pulpit, in that special place between God and congregation. It is hoped that in these few pages, contemporary preachers may find special appreciation for the blessings and burdens of their calling, as well as some ideas, anecdotes, even just a turn of a phrase or two, which shall be useful to them in their sacred work.

As in each of four previous books, an attempt is made to honor the art of preaching by offering a mixture of sermonic types. Concerning subject matter, some of these sermons are pastoral and spiritual in nature, while others are social and political. In the former case, the preacher's task is to enter deeply enough into his or her own strivings and shortcomings to connect with the strivings and shortcomings of the people in the pews. Spiritual and pastoral sermons are preached most effectively to others by honestly including oneself in the need and the message.

In the case of social or prophetic preaching, Biblical integrity requires the preacher to be political (for the Bible is certainly a political Book) but never partisan. Contemporary issues like values or violence must surely be treated from the pulpit in a transcendent, non-partisan, and trans-ideological way if the message is to sound like it comes from the timeless wisdom of God as opposed to the transitory cacophony of this or that party, crusade, or interest group.

More than their subject matter, the sermons in this book are also deliberately varied in style and structure. Good preaching requires a constant effort to stretch, to grow, to try out new formats and experiment with creative techniques. Some sermons can instruct in doctrine while others aim to convey an emotion or feeling. Some sermons can become dramatic character portrayals as seamless garments of storytelling, while others can conform to the requirements of classic "three-point" expository preaching. Some sermons can be light and humorous, while others can candidly address the most uncomfortable concerns imaginable. Sermons may vary greatly by type — this book tries to offer examples of each, thereby encouraging preachers to develop their own voices in all.

Still, discussions of homiletical subjects or sermonic structures are, in the end, merely technical and professional. The deeper hope for these sermons is much more dangerous and profound. It is hoped that preachers who read these pages may be encouraged in the difficult, often thankless, and frequently painful task of calling a congregation to be a church. It is hoped that all who read these pages may be encouraged to elaborate within their own Christian communities the biblical themes which can make the Church less beholden to the Grand Inquisitor and more beholden to Jesus Christ.

Lent is the perfect time for such a mission, for Lent is the one season in the liturgical calendar which offers preachers cover or permission to speak with the kind of honesty real repentance requires. The season begins with a searching of the soul, and proceeds through stories of doubt and betrayal until Christ's body is broken on a cross and then raised again in unfathomable glory.

For those who labor for God in Christian pulpits, seeking the renewal and re-empowerment of the Church, the message is direct and the model is clear. Indeed, the message and model are one, and for the sake of the Church's integrity and well-being, we can only hope there are thousands of prophetic men and women standing in pulpits across the land with the vision and courage to make it plain. Like Jesus Christ Himself, the Church which claims His name today shall find its glory not in its property or possessions, but in its poverty ... not in its proud privileges or resplendent rituals, but in its humility ... not in its cultural clout or electoral muscle, but in its weakness.

Erskine White
Nashville, Tennessee
June, 1997

Sermon
Ash Wednesday
Text: Matthew 4:1-11

Where The Spirit Must Live Or Die

"Then Jesus was led by the Spirit into the desert to be tempted by the devil." (Matthew 4:1, NIV)

In the months leading up to the day I was married, it fell on me to plan the honeymoon. I was living in a new city at the time and did not know the area very well, so I went to a nearby travel agent who booked us into what she said was a beachfront hotel just a few hours' drive from where I lived.

It *was* just a few hours away, but that was the only part of it the travel agent got right. The hotel turned out to be roughly akin to a trucker's hostel. The beach turned out to be black and rocky and littered with broken glass. Our room turned out to be a small cubicle in the basement, with no windows and a musty odor whose rancid memory still lingers. Needless to say, my new bride let me know in no uncertain terms that she was profoundly unhappy with this honeymoon experience; in fact, she *still* lets me know after all these years exactly what her thoughts are on the subject.

Tonight I feel like that travel agent, trying to convince you to go to a place you would never in your "right mind" choose to visit. I feel like I am saying to you, "Trust me: Buffalo is quite lovely in the middle of January!" or "Honestly, Houston is really the place to be during the height of the summer season!" As Ash Wednesday leads us into Lent, however, my job is even more difficult than talking you into Buffalo or Houston. Tonight, I must convince you to voluntarily and of your own free will spend forty days as Jesus did, being tempted and tested in the desert.

The desert Jesus knew is an awesome, forbidding place which looks more like a lunar landscape than anything from this world, stretching from Jericho all the way to Sinai and beyond. Its flat plains and jagged rocky hills have a severe beauty in their sun-baked hues of yellow and red, but the emphasis is on "severe." Here there is no hint of moisture anywhere except for the huge Dead Sea, whose water, as if by cosmic design, is the saltiest on earth and is in no way fit for human consumption.

For all its harsh and arid appearance, however, the desert is a profoundly religious place. It is no accident that so much of what we call the Holy Land is desert, nor is it an accident that so many people searching for God have found Him there. Hagar received God's promise when she was banished to the desert (Genesis 22:17), and Moses received the Ten Commandments there (Exodus 34:28). Other prophets from Elijah (1 Kings 19:8) to John the Baptist (Mark 1:4) heard God's voice in the desert and came storming back to civilization to repeat what they had heard. When Jesus went into the desert for forty days of testing and temptation, He followed sacred footprints which even the sands of time had not erased.

The desert is a religious place because it is a quiet place. So often, our communion with God is blocked by too much noise, shrill noises in the world and distracting noises in our hearts and minds. But in the desert, all you hear is the sound of the wind, and when that dies down, all that remains is the sound of silence. That is why God so often reveals Himself in the barren desert, where it is quiet enough for the human heart to hear.

Ultimately, the desert is a religious place because you can only do one of two things there: you can either live or die. You cannot just glide along in life as so many of us do, caught up in our daily affairs and going through the motions of secular routines without giving much thought to deeper realities or higher purposes. In the desert, illusions are stripped away and life is confronted on its most basic level. In the desert more than anywhere else, we finally come face to face with our ultimate helplessness and our utter dependence upon God.

If we cannot go to the actual desert Jesus knew in Israel, we are being asked to make that journey in a spiritual sense this Lenten season. We are being asked to put ourselves in a place where we must face our hungers and thirsts and confront our doubts and fears. We are being asked to abandon our pretenses, let down our defenses and allow God to challenge us with hard questions we normally avoid because we don't want to think about the consequences of our answers. The desert is a place where the human spirit must either die in despair or live exultantly in proximity to God, and we are being asked to test ourselves by going there.

Our searching and testing in the desert is a descent into honesty which takes place over time and proceeds in stages.

First, as the morning sun arises, we take a look deep within to examine our interior values and desires. We are put on this earth to "seek first the kingdom of God and His righteousness" (Matthew 6:33), and what untold riches would be ours if we lived our lives for that! Instead, we live for the things we earn by the sweat of our brow, being all too eager to "gain the world and forfeit our soul" (Mark 8:36), organizing our lives and our families for maximum material acquisition, fearing nothing more than even a slight drop in our standard of living and never understanding that we are ultimately owned by the things we seek to own.

We pay lip service to Christian values but live instead for the principles and pleasures of this world, making sure that the faith we profess does not require too much change or sacrifice from us. The divine voice within which would lead us to live by heaven's ways is drowned out by the relentless roar of our worldliness. On this Ash Wednesday night as we enter the spiritual desert of Lent, we must face the terrible possibility that we are faithless people living as children of darkness rather than as children of light.

The sun glows brighter and the parched desert plain grows hotter beneath our feet. Our thirst for faith burns within as we move from examining our own interior lives to examining our life together as a church.

We gather here as a people week after week to be the Body of Christ in the world, a "colony of heaven," a sacred community filled to overflowing with the power and love of Jesus Christ, and what a mighty witness we would be if we lived in that Spirit! Instead, we come to church as lonely, atomized individuals, keeping more to ourselves than we give to the community, seeking more to escape from the world than to be engaged in the world. We come here worshiping the convictions we already hold, pleased to have our opinions confirmed and annoyed when they are challenged in the name of the gospel.

We come here declaring our loyalty to Christ's church, but our levels of stewardship and mission show that our real loyalties are elsewhere. We come here claiming our identity as Christ's people, but disharmonies and disputations within the fellowship reveal a far less lofty identity. On this Ash Wednesday night as we enter the spiritual desert of Lent, we must face the humbling possibility that we are an apostate church, virtually indistinguishable as a community from the unchurched people around us and poor ambassadors of the One whose name we claim, our Lord and Savior, Jesus Christ.

At this point in our descent into honesty, we stop and protest that the judgment is too harsh, but the desert is a harsh teacher, and we do not enter it looking for glib reassurances or easy absolution! In the desert we learn that the depth of our sin offers no shade from the bright sun's searching glare, no rationalizations with which to justify ourselves. There is no place to hide as the sun climbs directly overhead and the shadows of our denial disappear. Our defenses grow weaker and our desire for God's Word grows more palpable as we move from examining ourselves as a church to examining ourselves as a nation.

Is this not the land which borrowed biblical language to call itself a "city on a hill" (Matthew 5:14) and a "light to the nations" (Isaiah 42:6), a land with "liberty and justice for all"? What a different nation and world this would be if our great power and prosperity were married to those noble purposes!

Instead, we are married to the marketplace, with its so-called "natural law" of competitive self-interest, a human-made law which can only divide and ultimately degrade a people. We are lost in the wilderness of misplaced priorities, generously subsidizing the rich, relentlessly squeezing the middle class, and moralistically "reforming" the poor by abandoning them to a "free" market system which exploited and profited from their poverty in the first place.

Meanwhile, on the global stage, we Americans are six percent of the world's people, owning thirty percent of its wealth. When you think about that single, telltale fact for a minute or two, and when you think about the sheer deprivation so many millions in the world endure, do we need wonder why, even now that the Cold War is over, we continue to spend far more on the military than all our enemies combined? Is it any wonder that our Air Force alone has more planes than almost every other nation on earth ... and this does not even count the planes our Army and Navy have!

Step back and see all this as the God of Scripture must surely see it. We are armed to the teeth like this, not to defend our national security, but to defend the imperial security of our unimaginably privileged place in the world — and woe to the politician or preacher who says that maybe too much is too much! So we go on, through Democratic and Republican governments alike, forging unholy alliances and relying on force as a first resort, trying vainly to postpone an inevitable reckoning with the moral compass of God's equity. As it is within our borders, so it is beyond our borders, and I, for one, say with Thomas Jefferson: "I tremble for my country when I reflect that God is just."

We suffer dangerous delusions as our technological prowess far outstrips our moral progress, and worse yet — the political and economic powers and principalities which govern us are completely unaware of their delusions! So convinced are we of our national righteousness that we dare to declare ourselves good and our enemies evil, not realizing that in God's eyes "there is no distinction" since all nations "sin and fall short of the glory of God" (Romans 3:23). On this Ash Wednesday night as we enter the spiritual desert of Lent, we must face the honest possibility that we are living in Babylon, drunk on power and dripping in blood, blindly lurching into a future which is gathering its forces against us, descending into hopelessness because we are spiritually unprepared to even *consider* the radical change of heart which might yet save us from ourselves.

Perhaps now our hunger and thirst for repentance have reached their peak, and as we finally see ourselves as we are seen by God, we come at last to realize our utter helplessness. Now there is nothing left to do but cry out from this blazing desert with all our might, "Help me, O God! Help us all! I cannot be faithful without You ... our church cannot be true to the name of Christ without You

... our nation cannot be saved without You." Now that we can confess our helplessness and complete dependence upon God, our growth as Christians and our journey to salvation can begin.

Jesus reached that point of helplessness in the desert, exhausted from His battle with the devil's temptations. At that point, our text says angels came and ministered to Him. When all He could do was live or die, angels came to Jesus to give Him the help and sustenance He needed, to shield Him from the desert sun.

We can trust God's angels to come to us as well. Yes, the purpose of a Lenten journey into the desert is to stare unblinkingly into the very depths of our sin, but we miss the point entirely if we fail to find God at the end of that journey, if we fail to hear His quiet voice speaking from the desert wind, telling us to believe in His mercy, promising to be there for you, for me, for our church and our nation because He knows we cannot live without Him.

Tonight we begin a journey which will take us to the wonder of an empty tomb. But first we must go into the desert, where our easy optimism and God-denying faith in our own devices are tested to the limit. We must go to dark Gethsemane and climb the hill to Calvary. Then and only then will we be ready for the glory of Easter Sunday, when an angel shall come and tell us that our hope which once was dead and buried has been raised to life again. Amen.

Pastoral Prayer

O God of all mercy and might, who calls us to a desert journey where we may encounter ourselves in all our despair and hear Your still, small voice of hope, we pray tonight for a sincere and meaningful Lenten experience. Do not let us pass through this special season as if it were "ordinary time," wrapped up in the small things which consume us and oblivious to the large things which can save us. Give us the faith to confront the truth within ourselves and the fortitude to stop living the lies which formerly have assuaged us. Take us into the desert where our Lord and so many others have gone before, subjecting ourselves to hunger and thirst, to trial and temptation, that we may learn our need for You, call upon Your name and be visited by Your angels.

Lord, embolden us to begin that journey tonight at Your table, where we receive food which never leaves us hungry and drink which never leaves us thirsty. Let this meal sustain us in the spiritual desert we must endure, O God, and help us pass the test which lies ahead, that in forty days we shall be ready to receive good news at an empty tomb, ready to live new lives as children of our Risen Lord, as members of His church and as citizens of this nation. In Jesus' name, we pray. Amen.

Sermon
First Sunday In Lent
Text: John 5:2-9

Giving Up For Lent

"When Jesus saw him lying there and knew he had been there a long time, He said to him, 'Do you want to be made well?'" (John 5:6)

I am afraid that this season of Lent, so rich in tradition and so pregnant with spiritual meaning, has become rather trivialized in the modern church, and nowhere is that trivialization more apparent than in the question Christians traditionally ask at this time of year: "What are you giving up for Lent?"

The popular idea is to abstain from something, to practice some form of self-denial or self-discipline for the forty days leading up to Easter. Given that we live in a culture which is utterly addicted to sensory pleasures and instant gratification, this certainly has some merit, but I wonder if we grasp the full meaning of the question as we decide what to give up for Lent.

For example, three young children showed that they were not entirely clear on the concept when they sat around the dinner table one night and solemnly announced that they would voluntarily and even cheerfully give up asparagus for Lent. When told that this didn't really seem like much of a sacrifice, they offered to deprive themselves, not just of asparagus, but of all the other green vegetables as well. Needless to say, their mother and I were unpersuaded, and your minister decided he still has some education to do in his own house on what it means to give up something for Lent.

We who are grownups generally understand that the idea is to give up something we like, not something we detest, but we really are not that much more spiritually mature than children, for we have developed our own ways of missing the point about Lent.

One of the most popular of our adult misconceptions about Lent is regularly demonstrated at Mardi Gras festivals. Every year in places like New Orleans and Rio de Janeiro, people take leave of their inhibitions in public debauchery right up to the very minute Lent begins, because once Lent begins, they have to give up all their swinging parties and sensual pleasures. For forty days, they have to be "religious," which means "dull" and "unexciting." Then, when Lent is over, they are finally "free" to have fun again.

Is this really what it means to give up something for Lent? Is Lent to be just a religious respite, an extended intermission, a forced "breather" during which we patiently wait forty days until we can get back to the "normal" lives we had before the season began? I dare say that the discipline of giving up something for Lent is supposed to mean far more to Christians than that.

In my own case, I might trivialize the meaning of this season by deciding to give up chocolate chip cookies, or trying to lose a few pounds during Lent. That would certainly do me some good, and in this age of physical fitness, many other people might decide to do the same. But here we are reducing the grand, expansive spiritual possibilities of Lent to the secular preoccupations of the day: our bodies and our physical appearance. Surely Lent is meant to do more than conform our lives to the ethos and program of the local health and fitness club!

The way we understand the phrase "give up something for Lent" shows how we tend to trivialize the meaning and miss the larger possibilities of Lent. We offer to give up (temporarily) our minor peccadillos and superficial vanities — turning down a cookie here, losing a few pounds there — while leaving unexplored the life-changing realm of spiritual rebirth and regeneration. The rewards we receive during this special season could be infinitely richer if only the things we gave up were infinitely more meaningful ... if only we didn't ask for so little and set our sights so low.

Our text this morning shows us a man who set his sights too low, a lonely invalid lying by a pool called Bethsaida, a pool with five porticos located near the Sheep's Gate in Jerusalem.

The man was there for a reason. Along with many others in Jerusalem who were sick, lame or blind, he knew the legend of the Bethsaida pool. It was said that every so often, an angel would come and ripple the waters of the pool, and that whoever then entered the pool first would be healed of whatever affliction they had. You had to be first, mind you — second place would not do — and you never knew when the angel would come; so, you can imagine how this host of desperate, needy souls would hover by the edge of the pool, waiting for the water to ripple and then trampling each other in a frantic effort to enter the water first and be healed.

One of the more interesting aspects of this text is the fact that you can go to Jerusalem today and see exactly where this story took place. You can actually stand on the spot where Jesus stood and encountered the paralyzed man by the side of the pool.

For many years, you see, this story was dismissed as a fable, a colorful miracle invented by the gospel writer to make a point about Jesus. But not too long ago, archaeologists began looking for Bethsaida's pool. Following the description in our text, they went digging near the Sheep's Gate in Jerusalem, and what did they find but an ancient pool! It had five porticos, just as our text says, and they also discovered why the water moved. It seems that the pool was fed by an underground spring which would periodically bubble up from below and cause the water on the surface to ripple.

I still prefer to think it was heavenly angels rather than an underground spring, but in any event, we do know that Jesus happened to visit this pool one Sabbath day and said to a pitiable man who was lying there, "Do you want to be made well?"

The question might seem strange at first, but it really isn't. People who suffer any kind of affliction, people who are troubled in any of a thousand ways must first be asked, "Do you want to be made well?" Do you want to be free of the torment which has burdened your soul all these years, or have you become so used to it that you cannot imagine its absence? Do you want to be made well, or has your suffering become an intimate friend you dare not let go, for fear you cannot function or even survive without it?

In a sense, the man by the pool was asked if he wanted to give up what was paralyzing him, and he answered by saying, "No." Rather than taking Jesus up on the offer to be made well, all he asked was to be carried to the edge of the pool so that finally, after all these years, he might at least have a chance of being healed by being the first to enter when the water moved.

He set his sights too low! It is like meeting the world's greatest tenor and asking him to sing "Row, Row, Row Your Boat." It is like meeting the world's foremost mathematician and asking her to balance your checkbook. Here a crippled, long-suffering man met the One who could heal him both inside and out, and all he asked of Jesus was to do something anyone with two strong arms and a healthy back could have done.

Somewhere deep inside, we all know we are like that man. We are all sitting alone along the crowded pathways of life as the healing waters go rippling by, each of us paralyzed by one problem or another, each of us hobbled in some way in body, mind, or spirit.

"Do you want to be made well?" Suddenly, Jesus is standing before us and catching us by surprise with this most improbable of questions. "Would you like to give up the inner wounds and spiritual struggles which are crippling your life, and start all over again without them?" Jesus poses the question, but we aren't yet ready to imagine our lives in those terms, so all we ask of Him is, "Please, Sir, just carry me over to the edge of my healing, so I might sit there and continue to dream that someday I shall no longer be as I am but shall be whole and healthy again."

"Do you want to be made well?" The question can be posed to each of us in an infinite number of ways.

To some of us this means, "Are you ready to give up your resentments?" For years, you have lain by Bethsaida's pool, harboring angry feelings about people or situations which have wronged you, or opportunities in life which passed you by. Friends have told you that these resentments are not healthy, that they twist your personality into knots of bitterness and rob your spirit of its joy, but they don't understand how badly you have suffered, nor can they right the wrongs or give you the restitution you deserve.

But now a Man is standing before you, asking if you want to be made well. Are you ready to give up the resentments which have crept in from the margins to poison the very center of your soul? It means being reconciled even though your cause may never be won or even recognized — are you ready to give up the raging resentments which have fueled your fires all these years and live the rest of your life with gratitude instead of bitterness?

"Do you want to be made well?" To some of us this means, "Are you ready to give up your guilt?" For years, you have lain by Bethsaida's pool, living with the brooding memory of things you did in the past, and it has hung over you like a permanent rain cloud on the horizon of your life. Other people have told you to forget the past and get on with the rest of your life, but you reply that this is easier said than done. They don't know how guilty you really are, or at least how guilty you really feel.

But now, a Man is standing before you, asking if you want to be made well. Are you ready to give up the crippling remorse which has tormented you for so long? It means letting go of familiar regrets and accepting the forgiveness which God and others have been trying to give you for years! Are you ready to trade your troubled melancholy for inner peace, and believe that the slate which once contained such damaging evidence against you has now been wiped clean?

"Do you want to be made well?" To others of us this means, "Are you ready to give up your self-recrimination and self-loathing?" Circumstances have conspired over the years to give you more than your share of burdens, and now you believe it was all deserved. Now you lay by Bethsaida's pool, convinced that no one else could possibly love you and certain beyond a doubt that God could never love you! The evidence for that is overwhelming!

But suddenly a Man is standing before you, asking if you want to be made well. Are you ready to give up your negative self-image and live in the positive glow of God's love? It means no longer seeing yourself as a child of dust tossed blindly to and fro, but seeing yourself instead as a child of God who is guided by His hand, for this is surely what you are! Are you ready to take the risk of actually giving up your lovelessness and believing in your heart that you are truly loved?

Finally, the question, "Do you want to be made well?" means for many of us, "Are you ready to give up your fears?" Are you ready to give up your fear of life and your fear of death, your fear of intimacy and your fear of loneliness, your fear of success and your fear of failure? It means no longer hiding anxiously in the safe shadows of doubt but stepping out boldly into the bright light of faith! Are you ready to give up all the apprehensions which have haunted your heart through the years, placing your trust in God and letting your faith in Him drive out all your fears?

"What are you giving up for Lent?" Suddenly the question doesn't seem so trivial any more. In fact, suddenly it seems rather silly to talk about asparagus or a few pounds off the waistline when we can talk instead about being made well — all the way down to the level of our deepest hurts and sorrows.

"What are you giving up for Lent?" We are giving up our inner resentments and guilt, our private self-loathings and fears — and anything else we harbor within us which hobbles our spirits, suffocates our souls and keeps us distant from God. We are no longer aiming too low with the things we give up for Lent, for now we are looking beyond the habits of the flesh to the habitations of the heart, where real growth and change most truly must begin.

In the weeks ahead leading up to Easter, we might want to think of this church, this sanctuary, this community of God's people, as our own pool of Bethsaida. Here we who are wounded and crippled in so many different ways have come to be made well in body, mind, and spirit. Here we have gathered to share our hope and seek our joy, to help each other move toward our healing as angels come by and ripple the waters.

Most importantly, here we may encounter a Man named Jesus who visits on a Sabbath morning, asking if we want to be made well and telling us not to ask for so little this Lenten season when He is offering so much. Trusting in His grace, we can reach for the goodness within our hearts and the heavens above our heads. We can reach for love, reach for peace, reach for God Himself, who has come near and is standing before us today, offering us His hand and telling us to stand. He sees us lying by Bethsaida's pool, our shoulders slumping under the melancholy weight of our need and sin ... now He is telling us to take up our mats and walk, for we have been made healthy and whole again. Amen.

Pastoral Prayer

Most Holy and Loving God, who asks that we give You not the sacrifices of ritual and custom but the sacrifices of our hearts and souls, help us to avoid trivializing this great and solemn season of Lent. Do not leave us content to ask so little of ourselves that we only give up the most superficial of our transgressions, the ones which scarcely touch the core of who we are and what we do. O God, help us to give up the most cherished barriers and break down the most intimate distances which separate our hearts from Your love. More than that, O God, help us to give up even our very lives for Lent — the lives we have led to this day — that we may live new lives in the manner of Him who is the Life, the Truth, and the Way.

God of all nations and Lord of history, we ask as well that nations and peoples everywhere give up in this Lenten season the political grasping and striving which causes wars and fighting around the world. Help peoples and nations everywhere to give up the selfish and callous greed which leaves privilege indifferent to human need. O God who is rich in mercy, open our eyes to the larger dimensions of change and repentance, that powers and principalities everywhere may stop waging war on Your Word and be servants of Your world, that Your peace at last may flourish and Your justice may finally be fulfilled. In Jesus' name, we pray. Amen.

Children's Lesson
First Sunday In Lent
Text: John 5:2-9

The Power Of Love

"Jesus said to him, 'Stand up, take your mat and walk.' " (John 5:8)

How many of you think your mother could lift up a car? Go ahead; take a look at your mother — or even your dad. That's right; there they are. How many think either one of them could lift up a car? *(Let them answer.)* Why not? *(Let them answer.)*

Well, those are all good reasons, and under normal circumstances I would agree with you: mothers, or even fathers for that matter, are not strong enough to lift up a car.

But every so often you hear about someone doing just that. I recall one story several years ago in which a young child was trapped beneath the wheel of a large car. His horrified mother came running over, grabbed the front of the car and lifted it right up off the ground, high enough for the child to crawl out from underneath the wheel. Then, when her child was safe, the mother couldn't hold it up any more, and it fell crashing to the ground.

Now, let's think about this for a minute. Why do you think she was able to lift up the car? *(Let them answer.)*

Well, I suppose you are right. Even though it seemed impossible to do, I think there are two reasons why she could do it. The first is that she didn't stop to think that she couldn't it. She didn't say to herself, "The car is too heavy," or "I am not strong enough to save my child." The thought of what she couldn't do never crossed her mind, so she was able to do what she had to do.

But the second reason is even more important, and it has to do with the mother's love. You see, she loved her child so much that she had this overwhelming need to rescue him. Nothing else mattered, not even her own life; in fact, she was aware of nothing else in the world but her child's need. With this powerful love, a special energy called adrenaline took over, and in an instant, an ordinary woman was picking up a 2,000-pound automobile, using only the power of her love.

Jesus was all the time showing people the power of love and, in the process, helping them do what they thought they could never do. He made blind people see. He made sick people well. One time, He even raised a dead man back to life because he loved the man so much.

In one other case, which I am going to talk about with your parents today, Jesus came upon a man lying in a street, a man who had been unable to walk for 38 years. Jesus asked the man if he wanted to be made well, and then Jesus said, "Stand up and walk." Now that poor man just knew he could not walk. I mean, he knew! Thirty-eight years had taught him that, but when Jesus said, "Stand up and walk," that man stood up and walked away.

You ask how Jesus did that? Or, you ask how He could make a blind man see, or a woman's dead brother come back to life? I honestly don't know. But I do know this. Jesus came to show us what God's love looks like in our world. And I know that as the mother showed us with the car, and as Jesus showed us in countless, even more amazing ways, we should never underestimate what the power of love can do. Amen.

Sermon
Second Sunday In Lent
Texts: Exodus 3:9-20; Romans 8:26-30

The Glory Of Our Weakness

"Likewise, the Spirit helps us in our weakness ... [interceding for us] with sighs too deep for words." (Romans 8:26)

A Baptist minister and a Catholic priest were playing golf one day, and the minister noticed that before every putt, the priest would cross himself. After nine holes, the priest was nine strokes ahead, so the minister asked if it would be all right if he crossed himself, too. "Sure, go ahead," the priest replied, "but it won't do you any good until you learn how to putt."

That little story says something about the way we value self-reliance in our culture. *"God helps those who help themselves"* — Benjamin Franklin said that, though most Americans probably think it is in the Bible! *"You've got to learn to stand on your own two feet; no one's going to hand you anything on a silver platter!"* Our language is full of aphorisms like that which underlie a harsh truth: we live in a society which treasures strength and self-sufficiency while detesting weakness and dependency. *"Pull yourself up by your own bootstraps like I did, and don't come crying to me, telling me your bootstraps are broken!"*

In fact, don't cry about anything, lest someone accuse you of being weak. Do you remember what happened to Edmund Muskie and Patricia Schroeder? They both ran for president, he in 1972 and she in 1988, and they both made the mistake of crying in public. Their credibility as candidates, with the press and public, was gone in an instant.

In hundreds of ways we can see every day, our culture abhors weakness. We are all supposed to be John or Jane Wayne, always strong enough to look out for ourselves and not needing anyone else in the process. But Christians know that John Wayne was

Hollywood, and that in the real world, we are not always so strong. Sometimes we are weak and feel totally inadequate to the challenge before us. Sometimes the deluge of life's difficulties threatens to drown us in the floodwaters of despair, and we fear we are going under. There is no shame in admitting that! It is part of being human.

There was once a man named Moses, who showed that even someone with great courage and strength can know his weakness as well.

He was living a rather ordinary life at the time. True, he had been through a harrowing adventure as an infant ... born of an oppressed race and destined for deprivation or death, his mother had taken him out of her run-down Harlem tenement into a posh Westchester County suburb and left him floating in a basket in a wealthy family's swimming pool, where the daughter of the president of the New York Stock Exchange found him and took him in.

And true, even though he had received all the material and educational advantages his adoptive family could give him, he had gone into hiding some years later after running afoul of the criminal justice system. He had killed a police officer during a riot which exploded in a pent-up, inchoate and collective rage after a young man who was pulled over for nothing more than "DWB" (Driving While Black) died in police custody. The charges against Moses were inciting violence and first degree murder, I believe.

But now Moses was married and settled down, living in an obscure town in upstate New York and minding his own business. Minding his father-in-law's business, to be more precise. Moses was in a small office taking care of the payroll and accounts receivable so his father-in-law could be out drumming up new customers.

One day, Moses was off on his lunch hour, jogging his usual 2.3 miles through the park, when suddenly he saw before him a bush which was on fire but was not being consumed. That is to say, this bush was full of flames, but none of the leaves were burning!

That got his attention.

Moses stopped to investigate this pyrotechnical contradiction when the voice of God spoke from out of the bush: "Moses, I have heard the voice of My people ... they are groaning under the weight of their poverty and discrimination, and I have come to help them. I want you to go down to Washington and enter the office of the Pharaoh, and tell that man to let My people go."

"Who am I," Moses asked, "that I could do such a thing? I am just a run-of-the mill payroll clerk in a small family business; how could I possibly be a match for Pharaoh? I don't have the right clothes, the right connections ... the Secret Service wouldn't even let me in the front gate, never mind into Pharaoh's office! I'm just not up to this, God; I think You picked the wrong man for the job."

"It doesn't matter who you are or what gifts you may have or lack. In fact, you don't matter at all, Moses! All you have to know is that I shall be with you when you speak to Pharaoh for Me."

"And who shall I say has sent me? When I tell my people that God has sent me to lead them to their long-awaited liberation, and they ask me who this God is, what shall I tell them?"

Moses looked down and saw a business card lying in front of the bush. It was embossed and glistened in the sunlight as he leaned down to pick it up, and there in plain black letters were printed the words, "I am that I am."

" *'I am that I am'*? Thanks a lot, God! I need a name that will impress my people and make them want to follow me. You know they are so flimsy and fickle that they could turn against me at any time. They are slaves who think like slaves — and You want me to tell them Someone named 'I am' has sent me to set them free?

"And while we're at it, what about Pharaoh and his people? Do You really think they will pay any heed to a God called 'I am'? Why can't Your name be 'Exterminator' or 'Ultimate Destroyer' — maybe that would do something to get Pharaoh's attention! No, the mighty Pharaoh in Washington doesn't respect weakness, God, and my knees will be knocking the whole time I am in his presence. I really wish You would find someone else to do this."

Moses felt inadequate to the challenge before him and looked for every possible way to excuse himself from it. Yet when God revealed His name to Moses, He told Moses all he needed to know:

"I am that I am." God is who God is, and because God is, we don't have to be all we think we have to be.

You see, when Moses or any of us tell God we are weak and incapable, we aren't telling God anything He doesn't already know! When we confess our frailty and finitude, we aren't exactly bringing a hot news flash to the ears of the Almighty! "It doesn't matter that you feel unequipped or overwhelmed," God said to Moses. "What matters is: My name is 'I am,' and I will be there with you."

The apostle Paul gives much the same message in our second text from Romans. The powers, principalities, and pressures of life may sap our strength and steal our courage, but they can never defeat us because "the Spirit helps us in our weakness." When we feel frightened and discouraged, unable to keep up in the contest of life's arena, that is precisely when God hears our cries as they rise to heaven and comes to help us in our weakness.

"Lord, I am a parent trying to raise my children in a fallen and frightening world. Sometimes I feel helpless in the face of everything out there which would lead my precious ones astray. From beer companies to peer pressure, from drugs to dropouts, from sellers of cigarettes and sneakers to peddlers of pornography and violence, there are so many demons out there trying to get their 'hooks' into my babies! And even if I can teach them to make the right choices and choose the right priorities in life, how can I feel good about the kind of world they will grow up to inherit? Where will I get the wisdom and guidance to raise my children today, when it seems that despite my best efforts, the siren songs of those who would seduce them are so stubborn and strong?"

The Spirit helps us in our weakness.

"Lord, I am aged and trying to live each day with dignity and grace. But I find it increasingly difficult to take care of myself, to do the simple things I once took for granted. I wonder how long my health will hold out, and how long I will be able to live in my home. I wonder how many losses of friends and loved ones I can endure before the loneliness overwhelms me. At a time in life when I need stability and security, I am facing more instability and difficult decisions than ever before. Where will I find the strength and stamina to survive my golden years?"

The Spirit helps us in our weakness.

"Lord, I am in business, trying to provide for my family and make my way up in this company. My boss just called me in and told me she wants to give me a promotion, putting me in charge of the whole region. I realize I should be happy for this opportunity ... so many people I once worked with have been 'downsized' and 'outsourced,' and I know good jobs are guaranteed to no one these days. Still, I wonder if I should do this. It would mean more money, which my family can surely use, but it would also mean I would be away from home even more than I already am. Right now I feel I have missed so much as my children grow up — why must I be made to choose between career and family? My boss says she needs my answer by tomorrow. Where will I find the courage to make the right decision?"

The Spirit helps us in our weakness.

How does God do it? Speaking in very concrete and specific terms, how does the Spirit help us in our weakness, when we face these and so many other dilemmas in life? The answer is: God helps us in more ways than we can imagine.

When you are a minister and the telephone rings in your home, you never know what the voice at the other end will say. From suicides to psychiatric breakdowns, from sudden deaths to domestic violence, I have been called into almost every situation you can think of, to be with people and families who are staring at the abyss and peering into the heart of darkness.

What do you think about saying as you rush to answer these emergency calls? What words will you offer; what sentiments will you express? How could *anyone* know the right words to say?

To be honest, I have never had a clue what to say. As I rush to the scene, I am acutely aware of my weakness and complete inadequacy. I know I am not at all equipped to be Christ's representative in the tragic, traumatic situations I am about to enter.

But then, when I am in the situation face to face, the words come out. Words which touch and heal, words which give hope and put painful problems in spiritual perspective. I know they don't come from me, for I know how frail and flawed I really am. In fact, I believe it doesn't even matter that I am there — what matters is that God is there — and that God can use any of His weak and inadequate servants to do what He did and said what He said in the midst of those crisis situations.

I dare say that you, too, have had experiences like that, where you were able to share the right word or gesture with someone else because it was given to you from somewhere beyond yourself. The next time it happens, be thankful for it! Remember how utterly inadequate you were, and recognize that this is one way God helps you in your weakness.

God also helps us by sending other people to be with us in moments of critical need. What happens when someone we know is faced with a medical crisis of some other shattering calamity? Do not friends gather around, offering to help in any way they can? What happens during unexpected disasters like plane crashes or earthquakes, fires, or floods? Solidarity displaces solitude. Strangers come together in an extraordinary spirit of sharing and selflessness which people rarely demonstrate during the regular course of normal daily living.

What is all this but God helping us in our weakness? It is God putting into people's hearts the desire to be present for others and rush to them with aid. The next time you are in a difficult situation and you see family and friends gathering around you, calling and visiting, sending cards and offering prayers for you, understand that this is another way God helps us at a moment in life when we are weak and needy.

"The Spirit helps us in our weakness ... [interceding for us] with sighs too deep for words." Sometimes there are no words to say or people to gather around us. Sometimes none of that is enough to reach the depth of our need. Yet even then, amid the silence and spiritual seclusion, God has ways of helping us in our weakness.

The story is told of a man whose little daughter was in the hospital, dying of leukemia. Daily he would visit her; on some days she was stronger than others, but her decline was irreversible.

Her birthday came around, and her father came into the hospital with a cake. As he turned the corner, he almost bumped into a nurse who was coming out of the chapel. He had been in that chapel many times before, a small room with a dozen chairs and a life-sized portrait of Christ on the wall. "How is my daughter?" he asked the nurse. She waited a long moment before she replied, "Oh, I guess you haven't heard. She's taken a turn for the worse."

Handing the cake to the nurse, he sprinted to his daughter's room, but it was too late. She was dead. Numbly, he sat there as the hours went by. People came and went, trying to offer words of comfort, but he didn't see them or hear what they said.

Finally, he got up to go home, and passing by the chapel, he stopped in. There was the birthday cake, with his daughter's name on it, sitting on a chair where the nurse had left it. He picked it up and pondered the absurdity of all that had happened.

Suddenly, blinded by his tears, he threw the cake at the picture of Christ, hitting Him right on the face. "Oh no, what have I done?" he thought to himself. "What blasphemy have I committed?" Then, through his tears, it seemed that the figure of Christ just stood there, allowing the cake to slide down His face. For a moment, the man thought he saw tears rolling down Christ's cheeks. The man felt as if the Scriptures were coming alive and speaking just to him: "[Christ] committed no sin ... When they hurled their insults at him, He did not retaliate; when He suffered, He made no threats" (1 Peter 2:22-23, NIV).

In some unexplained way, the man felt at peace. He felt that the heart of Christ was broken in sympathy for him. Mind you: no words were expressed — this man's anguish and sighs were too deep for words — but God was there, in the Spirit of His Son, Jesus, interceding for him and helping him in his weakness.[1]

Sometimes our illusions of strength and self-sufficiency are stripped away by things which happen to us in life, and we come face to face with our abiding need for God. At that moment, we find the glory of our weakness. We find that our weakness has truly blessed us by bringing us closer to God (Matthew 5:3).

When our cup is full, what can be added to it? Only when our cup is empty can God pour into it the living water of His love. Only when our spirits are punctured and deflated can God pump into us the renewing spirit of His succor and strength.

It says something beautiful and reassuring about the world in which people of faith live. When things are going fine, and we are filled with strength and vigor, we give thanks to God for our blessings and bounty. And when life's cruel blows rain down upon us, leaving us weak and needy, we still give thanks to God for blessing us with His presence and peace. Either way, we cannot lose. God is that God is. God hears our cries, even our sighs too deep for words, and He comes to help us in our weakness. Amen.

---

1. This story was originally told by Peter De Vries in his book, *The Blood of the Lamb,* and has since been recounted in several anthologies of sermon illustrations.

Pastoral Prayer

O Good and Gracious God, whose strength is both an awesome wonder and a tender word, we give You thanks today for our weakness, which draws us closer to You. Remove from us the conceit of believing we must be up to the challenge of every occasion. Teach us to rely less on our own devices and more on Your devoted love. When the odds against us seem long, remind us that You are strong. When we are tired and frustrated and ready to shed a helpless tear, remind us all that You are near. O God, help us to live more faithfully within the embrace of Your Spirit, that even in our moments of weakness and doubt, when our sighs are too deep for words, we may behold Your glory, receive Your grace, and praise Your holy name. We pray in Jesus' name, who taught us to say together, "Our Father ..." Amen.

Children's Lesson
Second Sunday In Lent
Text: Exodus 3:9-20

God's People Are The Little People

"The cry of the Israelites has now come to Me; I have also seen how the Egyptians oppress them." (Exodus 3:9)

How many of you have older brothers and sisters? *(Let them answer.)* If you do have older brothers and sisters, how many of you are also the youngest child in your family? *(Let them answer.)*

Now for those of you who are "the baby of the family," I want to ask you some questions. What is the best thing about being the youngest child? *(Let them answer.)* What is the worst thing about being the very youngest in the family? *(Let them answer.)* Actually, what I really wanted to ask is: how come the youngest child always gets the raw deal, the short end of the stick?

Maybe it's not true in your home, but in a lot of families, the youngest children feel like they are in a battle for their rights all the time. They feel that their older brothers or sisters don't treat them fairly. When it comes to deciding which television show to watch, who gets how many pieces of pizza, or who gets to sit in the front seat of the car — if these things were always left for the kids to decide by themselves, youngest children would never get their way! Am I wrong? Does anyone know what I am talking about here? Most times, the stronger ones get their way, and the smaller ones have to live with it.

Now, if *you* were the youngest child in that situation, what would you do? Who would you go to? *(Let them answer.)* That's right, you would go to a "higher power" — to mom or dad — to try to get some fairness, to try to get some justice. In fact, that is one of a parent's jobs: to try to make sure that all the children, even the youngest, are treated fairly. Parents have to make certain that the last in line gets to be first some times.

Well, a long time ago, the people of Israel needed help from a Higher Power. They were slaves in Egypt. They were worked hard every day building pyramids for the pharaohs. Their slave masters were cruel. They were hungry and beaten and suffering and dying.

Then God came to help, and He made Pharaoh let the Hebrews go. God brought His great power to earth, not for those who already had power, but for those who did not. Not for those who were strong and famous, but for those who were weak and invisible. God came to help the little people, because God's people are the little people of this world.

There are a lot of such "little people" in the world today. In fact, there always have been. They are all the people who are poor and hungry, all over the world and right here where we live. They are all the people who are out of work. They are all the people who do have jobs but are still poor, like the children who make our toys in faraway factories, or the people in our own country who pick the food we eat in the fields, or change the beds we sleep on in the hospital.

They are all the people caught in the middle of violence and wars — in countries like Ireland or Rwanda or Israel, and in our own cities and towns. They are the people who are hated because of their color or their religion or the accent with which they speak. They are all the sick and lonely and sorrowful and dying.

We tend not to pay attention to the little people. We tend to notice the big people, the popular, the powerful people. We put them on television and pay them lots of money and want to buy the same brand of sneakers they wear. If we had been visiting ancient Egypt, we would have noticed Pharaoh and the splendor of his magnificent court. We might not have noticed the Hebrew slaves at all.

But God noticed them. God showed that He is the kind of God who holds the little people of this world in a special place in His heart. As people have said for many, many years, God must really love the little people of this earth because He made so many of them. Of all the wonderful things we can say about God — all we could say about His power, His love, His Son and everything else — I think one of the most wonderful things to say about God is that He takes the little people and makes them His own. Amen.

Sermon
Third Sunday In Lent
Text: Jonah 3

The Day God Changed His Mind

"When God saw what they did, how they turned from their evil ways, God changed His mind about the calamity that He had said He would bring upon them; and He did not do it." (Jonah 3:10)

Repentance is high drama which is first played out in the arena of the human heart and then in the arena of the world. The drama begins with a searching look in the moral mirror of the soul. It intensifies to a searing moment of profound change and reaches its stunning climax with a response from God.

This high drama was played out in an Alabama courtroom a few years ago during a murder trial. The victim was a nineteen-year-old African-American named Michael Donald, who was brutally killed by two members of the Ku Klux Klan who had gone cruising the streets of Mobile looking for a black person to kill. Two years later, the Klansmen were convicted and sentenced to prison.

At that point, the victim's grieving mother might have been expected to issue a brief statement of relief and vindication, and then resume her life. But Beulah Mae Donald was not content with the two convictions. At the funeral, she had insisted on an open casket so the world could see what had been done to her son, and during the intervening two years, she had repeatedly criticized the silence of the Klan, which never issued a statement of regret. Now that the trial was over, Mrs. Donald still wasn't satisfied. In her mind, the court had not gotten to the root of the crime.

Her determination prompted some lawyers and civil rights activists to try a new legal attack on the Klan. Using what is known as the "theory of agency," they argued that the Klansmen who murdered Michael Donald were carrying out an organizational policy, and they sought to hold the Klan itself responsible, much as a corporation can be put on trial for the crimes of its employees. The idea was to hit the Klan where it hurt the most — to put the Klan out of business by bankrupting the organization.

She won her case. The all-white jury awarded her $7 million. The Klan had to sell its headquarters, and their members stood to have their property and wages seized. To the best of my knowledge, that particular branch of the Klan has never recovered.

Perhaps the most touching moment in this whole affair came on the final day of the trial, during the closing arguments. One of the defendants, James Knowles, rose to speak. "Everything I said is true ... I was acting as a Klansman when I did this," he began. "I hope you decide a judgment against me and everyone involved."

Then he turned to Mrs. Donald and looked her in the eyes for the very first time. He was weeping. "I can't bring your son back," he told her amid his sobbing and shaking. "God knows if I could trade places with him, I would. I know I can't. Whatever it takes — I have nothing. But I will have to do it. If it takes me the rest of my life to pay it, any comfort it may bring, I hope it will." By this time, everyone in the courtroom was in tears.

Mrs. Donald's answer was full of grace. "I do forgive you," she said. "From the day I found out who you were, I asked God to take care of you, and He has."

That true story shows the high drama of repentance in all three of its acts: act one is the inner struggle, act two is the visible change, and act three is the forgiveness. God took care of James Knowles by making him an entirely new man, and once Mr. Knowles became a new man, he received the forgiveness of the only person in the world who could give it to him.

All that is missing from this story is the larger dimension of repentance, the dimension found in our text from Jonah. Indeed, here we see the drama unfolding not only on the personal or individual scale we most often think of, but also on a national scale. The story took place in a distant land nearly three thousand years ago, but the lessons it offers to people and nations today are as current as this morning's headlines.

It is hard for us today to understand the scale of ancient civilizations, but Nineveh, the capital of the Assyrian Empire, was a colossal city located in the northern part of what is now Iraq. Jonah says it took three days to walk from one end of Nineveh to another; the city walls which have been excavated thus far are eight miles in circumference. When the palace library was discovered, it was found to contain tens of thousands of clay tablets. This was an imposing, impressive city in every respect.

It was also a very violent society in ways which might sound familiar to us today. Their sporting events and spectacles of mass entertainment dripped with violence. Their paintings and other forms of art were graphic in their glorification of violence. There was the overt and covert violence of a class system which kept some people subordinate to others. There was daily violence on the streets of a city in which weapons were everywhere.

Being a violent society at home, Assyria was also a violent society abroad; in fact, it ranks among history's most ruthlessly brutal empires. Surviving clay tablets actually boast of the mass-scale torture and genocide they inflicted on conquered cities, stories far too gruesome to repeat here.

As the greatest superpower of its day, Assyria imposed a world order which impoverished weaker nations and enriched itself. They subjugated foreign people and assassinated foreign leaders at whim when it suited their strategic interests. For a period of several hundred years, the Assyrian Empire earned the fierce hatred of much of the world, and when the end finally came for Nineveh, a Biblical prophet spoke for people everywhere when he exclaimed:

> *Woe to the bloody city,*
> *All full of lies and booty —*
> *No end to the plunder!...*
> *There is no assuaging your hurt,*
> *Your wound is mortal.*
> *All who hear the news about you*
> *Clap their hands over you.*
> *For who has ever escaped*
> *Your endless cruelty?*
> 　　　　　— Nahum 3:1, 19

Do we have any Ninevehs today? Do we have global superpowers or even regional powers in the world who earn the resentment of the weak by imposing their will on them?

I suppose the answer depends on where you live or what your perspective is. Many people might say Baghdad became a modern Nineveh, located as it is just a few hundred miles from the site of the ancient city. Depending on where they live, other people might name Moscow, Beijing, Jerusalem, or Jackson, Mississippi. Sad to say, millions of people in various parts of the Third World would accuse Washington, D.C. The world has always had its Ninevehs in one form or another, and we have ours today.

If you believe God created the universe, you also believe there is a moral order to the universe, since God would not create something that is amoral. In the case of ancient Nineveh and all the Ninevehs since, there is a certain inevitability about their fate because history is woven together by the thread of morality.

The pattern is familiar. Ninevehs expand and extend themselves into the world, using force to hold sway over more and more territory. They prosper for awhile, sometimes even for hundreds of years, because they are strong enough to take more than their share of the world's wealth for themselves. When they are at the zenith of their power and prosperity, they do not realize that they have already sown the seeds of their own undoing.

In order to preserve their privileged place in the world order, Ninevehs become ever more dependent upon their military might, devoting more and more of their resources to its perpetuation. They buy weapons they do not need and subsidize weapons which do not work. Other forms of national strength, such as economic, scientific, and educational power, are neglected, and eventually the imbalance reaches a point where a nation which appears outwardly strong is increasingly weak within.

Napoleon is said to have remarked to his Education Minister: "Do you know what astonishes me most in this world? The inability of force to create anything; in the long run, the sword is always beaten by the spirit."[1] Of course, Napoleon was merely echoing the ancient wisdom of Biblical prophets: "The war horse is a vain hope for victory, for by its great might it cannot save" (Psalm 33:17), and "Peoples labor only for fire; Nations weary themselves for nought" (Habakkuk 2:13).

Ultimately, that is what happens to Ninevehs everywhere — history records their descent as they lay their national treasure and the lives of their young upon the altar of empire's pride. They weary themselves into national exhaustion and finally come to nought, because the moral bankruptcy which went unnoticed for so many years made their material bankruptcy all but inevitable.

Our text does show an alternative future, however, even for as loathsome a city as Nineveh. It began with an action of God, who sent the prophet Jonah there to cry aloud in the streets: "In forty days, Nineveh shall be overthrown!" "Your evil ways contravene the moral code of creation, and God's judgment shall soon descend upon you." Jonah didn't even urge them to repent — he hated Nineveh too much to do that. He merely told them they were doomed.

The king of Nineveh might easily have looked at the panoply of power arrayed before him and laughed in disdain. "How is a God no one can see going to destroy all this?" he might have sneered. Instead, the king responded by repenting, and he ordered everyone else, even the beasts of the field, to do the same. Everyone great and small "shall cry mightily to God" and "turn from their evil ways and from the violence that is in their hands," he commanded.

Ninevehs are prone to delude themselves, thinking they are basically good and peace-loving at heart, and that whatever evil or violence they may commit are aberrations which do not reflect the real character of their national souls. The response to Jonah's warning allowed no such delusions. There could be no more violence at home or in the streets, no more profiting from violence in the arts and entertainment, no more violence abroad. Everyone from the king on down had to confront the unpleasant truth that violence is dripping from every hand, saturating society to its very core.

Then came the final act of this high stakes drama. As God saw an entire society changing its evil ways and repenting of its violence, He relented. God changed His mind and spared them the destruction which inevitably visits the Ninevehs of this world. Good leads to good and evil leads to evil in the moral universe of God's creation, but God is above even the most immutable law, so He decided in His love to suspend the rules.

Our text speaks of judgment, which is something the modern mind doesn't like to think about because we associate it with a vengeful and capricious God. But God is neither vengeful nor capricious. He simply created a moral universe, which really is the only kind of universe we could inhabit, and in that moral universe, good and evil must ultimately reap what they sow. Rather than being something to frighten or demoralize us, the Christian doctrine of judgment is actually our reassurance that God is in control of this tortured and turbulent world, and that God will speak history's final word.

Because God's judgments are His own and belong to no one else, it would be foolhardy in the extreme to think that Ninevehs only exist far away among our enemies and not also close to home. It would be far wiser to confess that the violent spirit of Nineveh lives here as it lives elsewhere, and to heed the warnings of the Jonahs in our midst.

In fact, God is calling on all who love Him to be modern-day Jonahs ourselves, to repent and change our own ways and to plead with others to do the same. There is subtle violence which poisons the heart and savage violence which pounds the earth ... "Repent of it all!" we must cry. "In our homes and streets and in the suites of power, repent!" Ninevehs everywhere need to know that someday it will be too late, that their vain and violent strivings are leading them inexorably to their ruin.

Too many Ninevehs have fallen in the past not to understand this. It is the moral compass of creation, the witness of history and the judgment of Almighty God. The Lord needs Jonahs today — will we answer His call or run away? The Lord needs Jonahs to live and spread His word, that people and nations may yet repent and give God a reason to change His mind. Amen.

---

1. J.C. Harold, *The Mind of Napoleon* (New York, 1955), p. 76.

Pastoral Prayer

Most Holy and Righteous God, who gave us a moral creation and who now grieves as we wound ourselves with sin, we confess today that there is evil in our hearts and violence in our hands. We find it all too easy to lash out and lack the strength to love. We find it all too easy to locate and condemn the other Ninevehs in the world but difficult to confess our own. God of all people, help us to hear the Jonahs in our midst, and lead us to be Jonahs for others as well. Stir within us and across the land a groundswell of repentance, a grand renunciation of violence in all its forms, that from the least of our citizens to the greatest of our leaders, from the neighbor across the street to the stranger across the world, we all may live as Your children, giving You good reason to change Your mind and alter the ruinous course we seem so grimly determined to follow. In the name of Jesus Christ, we pray for repentance today. Amen.

Children's Lesson
Third Sunday In Lent
Text: Jonah 3

The Things We Don't Want To Do

"The word of the Lord came to Jonah a second time, saying 'Get up, go to Nineveh, that great city....'" (Jonah 3:1-2a)

Everybody knows the story of Jonah and the whale, right? Every child who ever went to Sunday School has drawn a picture of Jonah being swallowed up by the whale, right? Well, not so fast: this is a story none of us know as well as we think we do.

First of all, we don't know it was a whale. Did you know that? The Bible never says it was a whale that got Jonah; it only says it was a "great fish." It might have been a whale, but it might have been something else, too. There are lots of animals and birds and fishes which used to live a long time ago, but now they are gone. They have long since disappeared. There are lots of fish in the deep oceans today and maybe even some animals on dry land which we have no idea about because we have never seen them. So the next time you draw a picture of Jonah getting swallowed up, use your imagination, because you don't have to draw a whale.

But here is something else: do you know why Jonah got swallowed up by the great fish? *(Let them answer.)* Well, the real reason is that he didn't do something the first time he was told to do it. God told him to go to a certain city and give a speech to the people there. God wanted Jonah to go and tell them to stop being evil and change their ways, or God would destroy them.

But Jonah didn't do that. The people in that city were enemies of Israel. They were vicious and cruel and everyone hated them — Jonah wanted them destroyed! He wanted them all to die! So, Jonah got into a ship and sailed off in the opposite direction because he didn't want to go where God told him to go and do what God told him to do. That's when the great fish swallowed up Jonah.

Well, Jonah started paying attention when he found himself inside the belly of a great fish. I guess that would get my attention, too. When he finally got out, he went and did the very thing he had not wanted to do the first time.

I'll bet you have lots of things you don't like to do or don't want to do. Some may be little things, like not wanting to eat your asparagus when your parents say you have to before you can leave the dinner table and watch television. Some might be really, really hard things to do, like when your teacher tells you to make up with someone you just had a bad argument with, and you don't want to make up because this person did something really rotten to you and you want to stay mad.

Well, I look at it this way. We all have things we don't want to do, but do you know what? We still have to do them! Sooner or later we have to do them! They don't go away just because we don't want to do them! They don't disappear just because we go off in the opposite direction and try to avoid them, like Jonah did. So, I figure we might as well get them out of the way. If you have a choice of eating asparagus or not watching your favorite television show, eat the asparagus first. Do the thing you don't want to do, and get it out of the way. Then it's not hanging over you. Then you can forget about it and enjoy what you *do* like doing.

There are many lessons in the story of Jonah and the whale ... oops, I mean Jonah and the great fish ... and here's a little one that is good. You can save yourself a whole lot of trouble if you do the things you don't like doing first. Amen.

Sermon
Fourth Sunday In Lent
Text: Luke 22:39-46

Christians Too Busy To Pray

"He came out and went, as was His custom, to the Mount of Olives ... [where] He knelt down and prayed." (Luke 22:39, 41)

It was bedtime for the six-year-old who had been sitting in the living room with his family. When his father told him to go up to bed, the boy immediately and without any protest headed for the stairs (which tells you that this story did not take place in my house), and as he reached the landing, he turned around and said, "Well, I'm going off to pray now. Anybody want anything?"

Of course, many people (and not just children) in this "gimme, gimme" society have that kind of attitude about prayer. Prayer is about asking and receiving, not giving and listening. It is the religious equivalent of going to the shopping mall, climbing up on Santa's knee and presenting a list of all the things we want.

Other people in our secular culture do not view prayer as a means to gain; they simply view it as irrelevant. I don't think I will ever forget how graphically this was illustrated one evening during the televised coverage of the 1988 Democratic National Convention. I was shocked as I watched this episode unfold on national television.

The incident took place during a pause in the speeches and as a minister was brought in to offer a prayer. The camera was on the Rev. Jesse Jackson, a candidate for president that year, who was standing on the edge of the speaker's platform with his head bowed as the prayer began. Suddenly, Connie Chung, a network news reporter, approached Jesse Jackson, intending to do an interview. At first, Jesse simply held up his hand as if to say, "Not now," but Connie Chung persisted with her question. Finally, the Rev. Jackson was forced to raise his head and say to her, "Please wait; we are praying now."

"They were only praying!" I suppose it was a perfect opportunity for an interview from a secular journalist's point of view, since there weren't any speeches being delivered and it wasn't time for a commercial yet. Certainly, listening to a prayer was far less important or newsworthy than getting Jesse Jackson's latest analysis of the latest issue on the convention floor. But from a Christian's point of view, that minister's prayer might have been the most important thing that happened all night!

Needless to say, we in the church know that prayer is not an exercise in "gimme, gimme," and we know it isn't irrelevant. Instead, the problem many of us have is that we are simply too busy to pray! We have so much to do and so little time in which to do it that we just can't spare precious minutes or hours sitting quietly by ourselves in daily prayer. That is a luxury we cannot afford. We Americans are a very practical, material, "results oriented" people who might feel we should be using that time more efficiently to accomplish something constructive.

Of course, the lives of great Christians have demonstrated that precisely the opposite is the case. I think particularly of Martin Luther, the Augustinian monk whose act of defiance against Roman Catholicism in 1517 launched the Protestant church.

Here was a man who preached weekly for his own congregation and wrote enough books to fill a good-sized library room from floor to ceiling. He corresponded widely with leading figures throughout Europe and often had to defend himself in the religious and political controversies which swirled about him. He was a devoted husband and a doting father to a large number of children, and when he wasn't occupied with all of that, he was busy changing the history of the Western world as a leader of the Protestant Reformation!

Luther was asked how, with all he had to do, he could afford to spend four hours every morning in prayer. His answer was that if he didn't devote that time in prayer, he wouldn't be able to accomplish half of what he was accomplishing with his life.

Just as physical exercise brings energy to the body, prayer is spiritual exercise which energizes the soul. A regular discipline of prayer does not facilitate a retreat from our busy world but a deeper engagement in it. More than that, prayer is indispensable for those who wish to pattern their lives after our Lord, Jesus Christ, who will forever remain the quintessential example of a Man who combined a life of action with a life of prayer.

Here in our text, we see Jesus in what must have been the most anguished, intense moment of His life. He is in the Garden of Gethsemane on the Mount of Olives, just a few minutes' walk from the city walls of Jerusalem and just a few hours away from His arrest, trial, and execution. He has come to this quiet place to pray.

The first thing our text tells us is that Jesus went to the Mount of Olives "as was His custom." This says that Jesus made prayer a regular habit, a customary pattern in the rhythm of His life. Indeed, even a quick reading of the gospels reveals any number of occasions when Jesus withdrew from His hectic schedule and the crowds which were clamoring for His attention in order to be alone and pray.

Because Jesus had prayed regularly for years, He could be helped by prayer when He needed that help the most. If you have not driven a car for ten years and suddenly find yourself driving in a dangerous blizzard, don't expect to summon up quick instincts and driving skills to save you, because you allowed those skills to atrophy through lack of use. In the same way, a prayer life which helps you through a difficult crisis cannot be summoned up or built in a day; a foundation must be laid patiently and persistently over the years until you have fashioned a structure of prayer which can withstand even life's most devastating storms.

The next thing we notice in our text is that Jesus approaches God honestly in prayer, making no secret of the way He feels. We are told that He prayed "earnestly," to the point where "His sweat became like great drops of blood falling to the ground." Picture a Man kneeling over a flat praying rock in a garden grove of olive trees, with darkness falling and deadly enemies just hours away. This was no time to try to conceal the way He really felt.

Of course, many of us do precisely that in our daily lives. Someone asks how we are and we breezily answer, "Oh, just fine, thank you," even though a voice is screaming inside that things are *not* fine. We put happy masks on our faces to hide our tears or distract attention from the tumult in our souls.

Perhaps we do this because we are too proud to reveal our weakness to someone else. Perhaps we were open with our feelings in the past and were stung by the indifference or betrayal we received in return. Maybe we think that a person with real Christian faith would not have such feelings, so we deny that they exist within us. For whatever reason, many of us have become quite skilled at hiding our feelings from others as well as ourselves.

Of course, we can hide our real selves from other people, but we cannot hide anything from God, and Jesus shows us that there is no reason even to try. After all, is this not the Son of God having second thoughts about going to Calvary? Is He not asking to be spared the cruel ordeal which lies ahead? *"Father, take this cup from Me!"* If even Jesus can confess His doubts and weakness when He comes to God in prayer, can we be any less honest when we enter the nights of our Gethsemanes? Indeed, there is no other way to be with God in prayer, because God knows what is in our hearts and minds even before we open our lips to speak.

Our text records only a brief, one-sentence prayer from Jesus, but that sentence represents the crux of a prayer which went on for hours: *"Father, if it be Your will, let this cup pass from Me!"* You have to imagine Jesus pleading with God long into the night, and then you have to imagine Him listening for God's reply.

Many people think of prayer as speaking to God, but as the years go by, I am more and more convinced that real prayer is a discipline of listening. The difficulty we find in prayer is the difficulty we find in listening, and if you wonder what I mean by that, go off by yourselves to a quiet place this afternoon and really try to listen.

What happens when we seek to listen in an attitude of prayer? As we wait for God to speak, our minds get filled with thoughts of things we have to do today, things we forgot to do yesterday or things which have bothered us lately. We get an itch on our leg and wonder whether to scratch it. There are a hundred barriers to real listening in prayer, and sometimes we can only manage to achieve a true state of spiritual listening for a few seconds or minutes at a time.

Nevertheless, this is what it means to pray, and Jesus listened for God's answer in the Garden of Gethsemane. Finally that answer came, and it is revealed in the second half of this one-sentence prayer in our text, when Jesus says to God, "Yet, not My will but Your will be done."

This is the end of every true prayer, for real prayer is not the discovery of our will but the discernment of God's will. Real prayer always leads us to say in one way or another, *"Thy kingdom come, Thy will be done, on earth as it is in heaven."* When you come away from prayer filled not with a sense of directing God to your purposes but being directed by God to His purposes, then you know you have really prayed, for you know you have really listened.

Notice that the answer is not the one Jesus asked for. God's will is rarely what we ask for, which is another test of true versus false prayer. Nevertheless, as soon as Jesus gets His reply — "God's will and not My will be done" — our text says an angel came from heaven and strengthened Him, giving Him the courage not only to face the trial which lay ahead but also to triumph over it.

That sequence of events in our text says a great deal about the power and efficacy of prayer. It tells us that in the end it doesn't really matter whether the specific prayers we make are answered or the specific petitions we ask are granted. What ultimately matters is being strengthened for life's journey, being "more than conquerors" (Romans 8:37) as we travel down life's road, being spiritually victorious in a way which does not depend on life's circumstances going well for us at any particular time.

For that, we need to listen as we pray, listen not for the answer for which we are praying but for the answer God is giving us. If God were to say to us, "I have taken care of the problem you have prayed to Me about," we may or may not be better off the next time a problem arises. But when God says, "I am with You," or "My will, not your will, is being done," then we know we are ready to face death and life, powers and principalities, things present and things to come, for God has given us — not the answer we may have asked for — but the only answer we really need.

I once knew a man who suffered painful arthritis in his hands, to the point where he could no longer do the things he loved to do.

As he prayed for years and years about his condition, his arthritis was never healed, but he did find himself growing in spiritual terms until he no longer felt debilitated by his disease. He became fond of saying, "I have arthritis, but arthritis doesn't have me!" Like Jesus in Gethsemane, he didn't get what he prayed for, but he was victorious in a more important way just the same.

The final lesson our text offers on prayer comes at the end, when Jesus warns His disciples to keep praying, lest they enter into temptation. In the disciples' case, they would be tempted to save their own skins when the soldiers came for Jesus — which is precisely what they did. In our case, we too are tempted to live for ourselves rather than Christ, even if in ways more subtle.

We can be tempted by materialism to live for our possessions and tempted by hedonism to live for our pleasures. We can be tempted by nationalism to hate our enemies and tempted by expediency to compromise our integrity. We can be tempted by privatism to live for ourselves and our loved ones, never understanding why this cannot be enough or why we are called out of our homes and into the household of God. Anything in life — be it within us or beyond us — anything which keeps us from living with God as our very first priority is a temptation, and Jesus is telling us to pray regularly that we may not enter into temptation.

I remember watching a young toddler at a party her parents were attending. She had obviously just learned to walk (for she careened around the room half in control and half ready to fall as early walkers do), and she was plainly delighted with her newfound mobility, but the room was full of very tall people she did not know. I watched her wander off exploring as children are wont to do, but she regularly came back to her parents (or at least came back to where she could see her parents), just to be sure they were still there. She didn't want to wander so far as to lose touch with them for more than a few minutes at a time.

This is how we are with God in prayer. As we wander off in our daily affairs, we need to check in regularly with God, to make sure we are not straying too far from His way, to make sure we are still in touch with His purpose for our lives and not living merely for our own selfish or worldly purposes. We need to be certain that the daily demands of our pursuit of happiness do not distract us from our greater pursuit of holiness.

Prayer is the way we do that. Prayer is our conscience checker, our reality tester, a lifeline which keeps us anchored to God's will as winds of temptation blow us to and fro. Prayer gives us strength for the journey while reminding us of our destination. There is simply no better way to remain focused on what is truly most important in our lives than to practice a regular discipline of daily prayer.

God is waiting to speak to us if we will merely take the time to listen. God is ready to comfort us in Gethsemane and guide us to eternity if we will merely seek His Word. It is for us a matter of vision, a question of priorities, a commitment to a quality of life far beyond our imagining. Yes, we all have long lists of things we must do today and every day, but can any of us say we are really too busy to pray? Amen.

Pastoral Prayer

Most Holy and Righteous God, who can speak through earthquake, wind, and fire, and who can whisper in a still, small voice which only a receptive heart can hear, help us this Lenten season to develop a more faithful habit of prayer. Teach us to seek You daily in prayer, first with honest confession, then with earnest petition, and finally with eager listening. Help us to trust that no matter how bruised or battered our spirits may be, You will receive us in our prayers just as we are, without one plea.

Help us, dear Lord, through the practice of daily prayer, to touch Your divine strength and grace, that we may be encouraged and sustained as we walk the crowded pathways of life. Speak to us tenderly as we listen for Your Word and tell us that Your will is being done, for then we may know a joy within us which triumph cannot flatter and tragedy cannot destroy. Build within us a spiritual edifice of power and truth, and let the foundation of that edifice be our daily devotion to the discipline of prayer. In Jesus' name, we pray. Amen.

Children's Lesson
Fourth Sunday In Lent
Text: Luke 22:39-46

Even Jesus Was Scared

"Then He withdrew from them about a stone's throw, knelt down, and prayed, 'Father, if You are willing, remove this cup from Me; yet, not my will but Yours be done.'" (Luke 22:41-42)

Last week we talked about Jonah, and I asked if you, like him, have ever had to do something you really did not want to do. Like eat asparagus. Well, this week, I am asking if you have ever had to do something you were really *afraid* of doing? Something that really scares you, and more than anything, you wish you could get out of doing? Like what? *(Let them answer.)*

Well, I know what one little girl would say! Every time her parents have to take her to the doctor's office, the first thing out of her mouth is always the same thing: "Will I have to get a shot?" It doesn't matter if they are going for a simple earache, a regular checkup for school, or even just to read the magazines in the waiting room: she is terrified that just by walking in the door of the doctor's office, some law says she will have to get a shot!

The other day she was asking her dad to tell her exactly how many immunization shots she will have to get between now and the time she turns sixteen. Of course, her dad had no clue, but that did not stop her from asking a zillion questions anyway. "How many measles shots do I get?" "What's a typhoid?" "How many typhoid shots do I have to get?" "When do I have to get another polio shot?" When her father probed his memory banks and said he thought the polio medicine came inside a little sugar cube, she felt a little better, but she still was very unhappy about the whole thing. You see my nine-year-old daughter really, really hates shots!

We all have things we hate doing, things that frighten us, things we would do almost anything to avoid. You might be surprised to find out that Jesus did, too! Yes, when He got near the time when

He knew He would be arrested, and suffer a terrible, painful death, He was scared, too. Plenty scared.

So, He did what a lot of people do when they get scared: He prayed to God. And He told God exactly how He felt. Jesus said He did not want to go through with it. If there is any way, He said, for Me to just walk away from here, retire from all this turmoil, not get arrested and put to death, and live quietly somewhere for a long, long time, please tell Me now. You'd better tell me quickly, God, for the hour is late. It is a bitter cup I am about to drink, Jesus said to God; if You can take this cup away and save me the suffering I know is coming, just do it.

But in the end, Jesus did what He had to do. He had to suffer and die so He could rise again from the dead, and give us all life forever in heaven. Jesus was scared, yet still He said to God, "God, if it were My choice I would not go through with this, but it isn't up to Me, it is up to You. If You say I must, then I will."

There is a rock opera called *Jesus Christ Superstar*, where Jesus sings, "God, Thy will is hard/but You hold every card...." That is what Jesus said as He prepared to suffer and die: "God, not My will, but Your will, be done."

A lot of times, we get scared in life, and adults know this as well as children. Even the bravest soldiers are scared going into battle. Even the bravest police officers and firefighters are scared when the sirens ring and they race off to an emergency. Even the bravest mothers are scared when they go into the hospital to give birth to a baby.

Listen carefully, children: courage does not mean not being afraid. People with courage get scared all the time. Courage means doing what you have to do *even when you are scared*. That is what courage really means! So you see, when you are scared about getting a shot, it doesn't mean you aren't brave. Everyone gets scared of something — you show real courage when you get the shot anyway, despite your fears! Just like Jesus, for He went on and did what He had to do anyway even when He Himself was scared. Amen.

Sermon
Fifth Sunday In Lent
Text: Matthew 27:15-26

Barabbas Speaks

"At that time, they had a notorious prisoner, called Jesus Barabbas." (Matthew 27:16)

Have you ever watched someone else die in your place? Have you ever stood by and watched another man die a slow, agonizing death, knowing all the while that you were supposed to be the one suffering and dying, not him?

I have. It happened many years ago when I was a prisoner of the Romans in Jerusalem. I was scheduled to die by crucifixion, but at the last minute, they set me free and executed another man in my place. That man's name was Jesus, the One you call Christ.

I have to be specific about what this other man is called because my name is also Jesus — Jesus Barabbas.[1] Of course, this coincidence became supremely ironic on that first Good Friday in Jerusalem, because there was that bloodthirsty snake, Pontius Pilate, presenting two men to the crowd, saying one would live and one would die ... and what was he doing but presenting two Jesuses who were as different as night and day! "Which Jesus do you want," Pilate asked, "Jesus Barabbas or Jesus who is called the Christ?" The crowd had to choose between us and decide which Jesus they would follow. Needless to say, they chose me.

I do intend to tell you what happened that day, but first, I must explain myself to you, because I really feel you Christians have judged me too harshly over the years. You read the gospels, where I am called a "notorious prisoner" (Matthew), a "murderer" (Mark and Luke) and a "robber" or "thief" (John), and you think I was some street criminal like the ones you see on the evening news. Well, did you know that the same Biblical word for "robber" can also be translated "revolutionary"? Indeed, that is what I was! Perhaps now you will dig beneath the stereotypes and get to know the truth about me, because there is more to the story of Jesus Barabbas than what you have previously heard!

My name, Barabbas, means "son of the teacher" (or rabbi).[2] Yes, my father was a rabbi, a very learned man, which means I was raised in a fairly well-to-do, comfortable home where education was both a privilege and a duty. My father taught me the stories of our faith and the glories of our nation's past, the stories of great heroes like Daniel and Deborah, Joshua and Jael. I heard them so often that they finally became a part of me.

Of course, my favorite heroes were King David and Solomon, because they ruled when Israel was a mighty empire. Our cities were magnificent, our borders stretched from Mount Hermon to the Negeb, and foreign leaders like the Queen of Sheba came to us for trade and diplomatic relations. Our temple in Jerusalem rivaled any in the world. It was Israel's Golden Age, and my father's chest swelled with pride when he told me about it. He taught me to love God and my country. Is that really so bad, and do you not teach your own children to do the same today?

Needless to say, Israel's Golden Age was but a distant memory by the time I was born. Our nation was occupied and governed by the Romans, who gloried in their empire and their so-called "civilization" but were really butchers and barbarians at heart. They elevated cruelty and exploitation to an art form, controlling our lives, robbing us blind with punitive taxes and crushing even the mildest rebellions with prison terms, torture and execution. I tell you: it is hard to describe the humiliation, the hatred, and the anger we felt for these Romans dogs! Anyone who loved God and Israel — indeed, anyone who possessed even half a conscience — had a decision to make, and I made mine.

I suppose I could have tried to ignore the pain my country was suffering; I could have settled down, married a nice Jewish girl, and carried on with the safe, comfortable life of a rabbi's son. But as the Scripture says, "The fear of the Lord is hatred of evil" (Proverbs 8:13), and I hated Roman evil as much as I feared God. My sense of outrage against injustice, my yearning for the day of the Lord, and my patriotic fervor burned too hot in my breast, and I knew I had to resist the Romans. I knew I had to go to war.

I joined a group of religious revolutionaries called the Zealots. We didn't have the resources to fight in the open, so we used the weapons of sabotage and terror, much as those whom you call "terrorists" fight today. For this, of course, the Romans condemned us, but it was all so hypocritical. Isn't it funny how the world's superpowers can profit from injustice and terrorize other nations with weapons of unimaginable destruction, but when weaker parties like us fight back with the only weapons we have, we are called "immoral" and "criminal"! The robbery of the strong is "law and order" while ours is "terrorism." Oppressors never understand moral hypocrisy as clearly as those whom they are oppressing.

Our mission as Zealots was to kill Romans when they weren't looking and then disappear before they could catch us. We wanted them to live every day in fear, never feeling safe and never knowing where we would strike next. And, of course, we took an oath to kill every Jewish tax collector in Israel, since they were collaborating with the Romans and getting rich in the process.

The first Roman I killed was a centurion standing guard at the temple. I snuck up behind him and ran a long knife through his back and out the other side, and quite frankly, I never thought twice about it. These Romans were butchers, and the mere thought of them filled me with more than enough hatred to kill. Why, I no more regretted taking a Roman life than I would regret killing an insect or doing away with a bothersome rodent.

Besides, we were soldiers of Almighty God. Our cause was just, our struggle was sacred, and we prayed for the day when God's Messiah would come to drive the Romans out of Israel and into the Mediterranean Sea. My comrades and I became closer than brothers as we risked our lives together and depended on each other to stay alive. We were freedom fighters and heroes to the people, since we were brave enough to do what they only wished they could do.

You need to know all this to understand what happened on that momentous day in Jerusalem when the fate of two men named Jesus was decided. Pilate offered to release one of us and asked the crowd to choose.

Of course, my comrades were in the crowd, telling people to call for Jesus Barabbas. But I dare say that even without my friends there, the crowd would have chosen me anyway. In fact, I dare say that were the same choice offered to a crowd of your fellow citizens today, they would still choose me!

You condemn me for being murderous and violent — for being Barabbas — but in the end, I am not so very different from you. When you buy toy guns and swords for your children to play with, what are you giving them but the tools of my trade? When you go to the movies and watch Hollywood "heroes" spew rivers of blood across the screen, what are they doing but playing the part of Barabbas! In a way, it's too bad I was born so long ago, because I could have made a fortune in a culture like yours!

Your leaders speak eloquently of justice and peace, but do you not depend on threats and violence to get your way in the world? You go to war often — more often than most nations, in fact — and when you do, do you know or even care how many of the "enemy" you kill? Do their lives matter as much to you, and how is this different from my own casual conscience about killing Romans? At least Barabbas can say he killed his enemies in the cause of freedom; can you say that all of your wars are fought for such high and noble purposes today?

Yes, don't condemn me too quickly, and don't condemn the crowd in Jerusalem for choosing me over the other Jesus, because the truth is: you know Barabbas all too well. You subscribe to my methods and values all too easily, and you are more like me than you care to admit. The world may admire people of faith, but it pledges its allegiance to people of force, and I was counting on that as Pilate stood between your Jesus and me with our lives hanging in the balance. I knew all along that He would be crucified and I would be set free, because that is the way the world has always wanted it to be.

People have often asked me how I felt as I watched Christ's life being ransomed for my own. To be honest about it: I looked over at your Jesus and thought to myself, "What a fool He is! How is His philosophy of charity and peace helping Him now? The people He talks about forgiving are screaming for His blood! The Romans whose evil we are supposed to resist with love are preparing His crucifixion! Why, if it were up to Christ to decide between us,

He would volunteer to die in order that I — a violent Zealot who repudiates everything He stands for — might live! How could anyone be so foolish as to think they will actually get ahead in this world by putting the needs of others above their own?"

I can't say I felt sorry for your Jesus as they led Him away, although I did shudder at the torture I knew He would endure. You who are so far removed from my era may not realize how cruel and agonizing a Roman crucifixion really was; people often hung on their crosses for many hours and even days, racked with pain and wishing that death would come. It was just one more reason to hate those barbaric Romans and give them what they deserve.

When the Romans released me, my friends wanted to celebrate, but I had to go to Calvary first. Not to see Jesus, mind you, but to be with the other two men who were crucified that day, the two men I was supposed to die with. They were Zealots like me — my friends, my brothers in arms — and comrades like us do not desert one another even in the worst of times. It was the least I could do, and it was more than the followers of your Jesus did for Him, I might add! *"Were you there when they crucified our Lord?"* It is hard to describe the contempt I felt that day for the disciples of your Jesus who saved their own skins by running away.

Those were my feelings many years ago when I was a young, hard-bitten revolutionary who gave no pity and asked for none in return. I was convinced beyond a doubt that my language of brute force, and not Christ's language of love, is the only language this world respects, the only vocabulary this world can understand.

Now I am not so sure. First, I began to question the effectiveness of the tactics I once espoused. Not too long after Christ's death, my fellow Zealots launched an all-out war against Rome, which resulted in the total destruction of our country and the scattering of our people to the winds. It was a national disaster, and all our violence did was precipitate more violence.

By contrast, Christ's church flourished despite Roman persecution which was as fierce and relentless as anything we Zealots faced. Their only weapons were steadfast faith and suffering love, but see how they succeeded! Today, the vaunted, invincible, "eternal" Roman Empire is nothing but broken stones and crumbling ruins while the Christian church lives on in every corner of the earth. Maybe it's true that things like worldly power, prestige, status and wealth must wither and die while spiritual things abide. Maybe it's true that violence begets violence, and real peace can only be won by peaceful means.

I also began questioning myself when I saw how people I knew were changed by this Jesus of yours. One of His disciples was a tax collector named Matthew, a collaborator with Rome, and another disciple was a Zealot named Simon, who had sworn an oath to kill all tax collectors. Imagine a tax collector and a Zealot becoming spiritually bonded under one Lord! Imagine the former laying down his ill-gotten riches and the latter laying down his sword! Maybe it really is true that hatred defeats us by making us become the enemy we despise, and only love can save us.

I know I am not sounding much like Barabbas any more, and it bothers me to say things like this. But in the end, my doubts about my former life came down to a very personal struggle. I could not shake from my mind the sight of that other Jesus as they led Him away to be crucified. Most men who are innocent and about to die for a guilty man would be screaming out in helpless rage. This Jesus merely looked at me with kindness and generosity in his eyes, as if to say, "You have your life back, Jesus Barabbas; now decide what you will do with it."

He died in my place and gave me a second chance to live. That fact has haunted me ever since, but I am here to say that it should haunt you as well. You should wrestle with the implications as intensely as I have done because, you see, Jesus Christ didn't just die in my place on Calvary's hill; He died in your place, too.

Can you see yourself as Barabbas, ready to die in your sin as I was ready to die in mine? Each one of us would be crucified on the cross of our own unrighteousness if He had not been willing to take our place; can you understand that Christ died as much for you as for me? If you can, then you are ready to take a hard look at the priorities in your life and the values in your heart. Like all people who have a close brush with death, you are ready to see everything differently now that you have a second chance at living.

Suddenly I am not so sure about the ways, the means, and the ends to which I devoted myself in the past. Suddenly I wonder if I haven't been wasting my life whoring after worldly visions of might and right which deceive and finally destroy. A Man took my place on the cross and gave me a new life to live. My friends may be surprised to hear me say this, but I, Jesus Barabbas, intend to do the best I can with the second chance I have been given. What will you do with yours? Amen.

---

1. Some ancient versions of the Gospel of Matthew, including the Syriac and Armenian versions, give Barabbas' first name as Jesus.

2. Bar-Abba means literally, "son of the father," while variations of the name as recorded in certain ancient manuscripts include "Bar-rabban," which means "son of the teacher" (or rabbi).

Pastoral Prayer

God of the heavens and Creator of all worlds, we are trying to be like Barabbas today, reflecting on the infinite meaning of Your Son's sacrifice upon the cross. We examine our lives and assess our consciences, asking ourselves how much of them are worthy of our Christian faith and pleasing to our Lord. We question the extent to which worldly goals and values matter more to us than faithful service and heavenly rewards. We confess that in more ways than we would like to admit, there is a Barabbas within each of us who can only be grateful that Christ has come to die in our place, that we may no longer be condemned by our sin.

Make that sense of gratitude rise up within us like a mighty flood of righteousness, O God, that we may take full advantage of our second chance in life. Where we have been petty and spiteful, make us generous and serene. Where we have been quick to withdraw and condemn, make us eager to embrace and communicate. Where we have been silent in the face of wrong, make us vocal in the cause of right. Where we have passively accepted the savagery of war and violence, make us militant in the sacred struggle for peace.

O God, as Christ takes our place on the crosses of our sin and sorrow, grant to us a new vision of life as You intend it to be lived: in faith which leads to joy, in courage which leads to hope, and in grace which leads to love. Amen.

Children's Lesson
Fifth Sunday In Lent
Text: Matthew 27:15-26

Jealous Of The Good

"For he realized that it was out of jealousy that they had handed Him over." (Matthew 27:18)

When the Romans ruled Israel at the time of Jesus, they had an interesting custom about this time of year. A crowd of people would gather in front of the governor, and they could vote on releasing any prisoner they wanted from prison. It could be a murderer, a thief, a terrorist — anyone. Every year at this time, one person put in prison for a crime would be given his freedom, and the people got to choose which prisoner that would be.

What do you think about that? Do you think that is a good idea? Do you think we should do that today? *(Let them answer.)*

Well, when Jesus was arrested, He was one of the prisoners who could have been released. But there was another prisoner in jail at the same time named Barabbas. The governor brought out Jesus and Barabbas and asked the crowd which one should be set free. The people voted for Barabbas to be released, and he was. They didn't choose Jesus, so He was taken away to be crucified, to be put to death on a cross.

Why did they choose Barabbas and not Jesus? Barabbas had killed people; Jesus had only helped people. Jesus had never done anything bad or mean in His life, but the people wanted Barabbas set free instead of Jesus. Why do you think that was?

The Bible only gives one very vague reason. It says the people voted to free Barabbas because they were jealous, but it doesn't tell us *why* they were jealous of Jesus! Maybe they were jealous because Jesus was so popular. Maybe they were jealous of Jesus' power, that He had the power to heal the sick and make the blind see and make the people who were discouraged feel hope again.

Maybe they were just jealous because Jesus was just such a good person in so many ways.

Don't think the people in that crowd were so different and terrible, because we get jealous for the same reasons today. We get jealous of the people who do something really well, like in school. We get jealous of people who seem to have perfect grades, or perfect families, or perfect lives. We get jealous of people who do a lot of good for others. "Oh, I'll bet they're really not all that good," we say to ourselves. "I'll bet they're faking it; I'll bet they really aren't as good as they make us think they are."

When you see someone else doing something really well, when you see someone else being really good and doing good things and making everyone talk about them and praise them — don't get jealous! Find out how they do so well and try to be like them, but don't get jealous of them! Being jealous of people who are good can make you do or say really bad things, things that deep in your heart you do not want to do or say — like what happened so long ago when a crowd of people got jealous and voted for a killer named Barabbas instead of a Savior named Jesus. Amen.

Sermon
Palm Sunday/Passion Sunday
Texts: Isaiah 50:4-9a; Mark 11:1-10

The Strength To See It Through

"The Lord God helps me ... and I know I shall not be put to shame; He who vindicates me is near." (Isaiah 50:7)

Things are not always as they seem, and this may be more true on Palm Sunday than any other day of the Christian year. Today we have celebrated the superficial meaning of Palm Sunday by parading into church waving palms and singing praises. The deeper meaning of Palm Sunday has yet to be revealed.

Superficially, Palm Sunday is as our text from Mark describes it: we are told what happened that day, what Jesus saw with His eyes and heard with His ears as He entered Jerusalem. But our other text from Isaiah tells us what Jesus felt in His heart and knew in His mind, and this is where the real drama of Palm Sunday unfolds. This is also where Palm Sunday becomes not just an event to be remembered from the distant past, but a profound spiritual lesson for the living of our own lives today.

As Mark recounts it, Palm Sunday is a day of joy and jubilation. Jesus is coming to Jerusalem as the Old Testament prophets had said the Messiah would come: riding on a donkey (Zechariah 9:9-10) and appearing at the Golden Gate on the eastern side of the city (Joel 3:1-12). The cheering crowds are filled with excitement as they spread their coats and leafy palm branches on the road before Him. Shouts of "Hosanna!" (which means "Save us!") fill the air, and the people are calling Jesus their king. Judging by what the eye can see and the ear can hear, Palm Sunday is a festival, a street party, a day of promise and celebration.

For someone like Jesus, who has been embroiled in controversy since the day He was born, it must have been a day of vindication and validation. To hear your praises sung when so many people have condemned and rejected you is a high moment indeed.

But as is so often the case in life, the real meaning of a situation lies beneath the surface and paints a different picture. In this case, even as Jesus receives the adulation of the crowd, He knows what is coming. He knows that in just a few days, the cheers will turn to jeers and the hosannas will descend into hisses. This is not Palm Sunday for Jesus so much as Passion Sunday — not the culmination of a triumph but the commencement of a test which will only grow more severe during the week which lies ahead.

Do you ever wonder what Jesus was thinking as the cheering crowd surged around Him and swept Him into the city? It would have been entirely natural and perfectly human on His part to let His mind drift back a few centuries to the prophet Isaiah. After all, when we have certain problems today, we join support groups with other people who share our experience; so might our Lord have sought support in the words of a prophet who had experienced in some measure what He Himself was about to endure.

In Isaiah's case, he tells us in our text that God has given him the tongue of a teacher and preacher, that he may "sustain with a word" those who are weary. He listens daily to hear what God would have him say, and then the prophet "does not rebel" or "turn backward" — he goes forth and gives the people the message which God has given him to speak.

To preach God's word courageously is always a hazardous duty, and Isaiah is no stranger to the consequences. He says he is physically attacked by people who strike him, insult him, and spit upon him (v. 6). He is also emotionally attacked by people who hide in the shadows, gossiping and criticizing him amongst themselves from the safety of anonymity, people who refuse to "stand up" and "confront" him face to face (v. 8).

The book of Isaiah as a whole makes it clear that the people of Israel have two main complaints against him. First, they find his preaching offensive. They are offended when he condemns their nation's leaders (chapter 28), the unjust policies of their government (chapter 10), and their reliance on the strength of their army (chapter 31). The men are offended when Isaiah denounces their idolatry (chapter 44), and the women are offended when he criticizes their moral complacency (chapters 3 and 32). Across the board, the good people of Israel want a preacher who will pander to them, who will tell them what they want to hear and affirm the values and ideologies they hold most dear. Woe to the preacher whose faithfulness to God fails to oblige the people!

Their second complaint against Isaiah can be stated like this: "You care for newcomers and strangers we don't even know as much as you care for those of us who have been God's chosen all along." To the dismay of a people who want to believe they are uppermost in the mind of God, Isaiah continually looks outward to "all people" and "all flesh" (*e.g.*, 40:5, 49:26, 66:23), rather than confining his ministry solely to the existing congregation of Israel.

Of course, Jesus could identify with all of this, since He, too, offended people with His preaching and He, too, ministered as much to the Gentile/outsider as the Jew/insider. Jesus could also identify with the way Isaiah responded to his critics: "I gave my back to those who struck me," Isaiah says in our text, "and ... I did not hide my face from insult and spitting." This will be Jesus' way as He suffers His Passion in the coming week, and I suspect our Lord may well have found comfort in the words of an ancient prophet who had gone that way before Him.

There comes a time in the life of every servant of God when the will to continue is sorely tested. The criticisms cut too deep, the cost seems too high, the controversies seem too much to bear. The loneliness seems overwhelming and the desire to quit the ministry God has assigned is most alluring. Isaiah knew that feeling, and Jesus may have flirted with it on Palm Sunday as He watched a fickle crowd cheer His name, knowing how soon they would turn against Him with a savage fury. Jesus surely knew the feeling on Maundy Thursday as He prayed in the Garden of Gethsemane, and on Good Friday as He hung on a cross to die.

But at that very moment, when the temptation to give up is strongest, God draws near to His servant in a way which sustains the flickering spirit. God somehow enters the weak and hurting heart, and resignation instantly gives way to resolve. Suddenly, and "in the twinkling of an eye" (1 Corinthians 15:52), someone who was ready to quit God's service now feels ready to take on the world.

This is certainly what we see in Isaiah, who is able to tell his adversaries, "[But] the Lord God helps me ... and I know I shall not be put to shame." It is a sense of God's presence and care which fills the prophet with a mysterious courage and then allows him to say to all who will hear, "Who are my adversaries, and who will contend with me? Let them step out of the shadows and stand here with me. Let them confront me face to face, for it is the Lord God who helps me, and He who vindicates me is near."

Jesus may well have drawn upon such reassurances as He looked at the crowd around Him and contemplated what lay ahead during the ordeal we call Holy Week. Surely He was not fooled by the flattery of their Palm Sunday cheers, and if He was comforted by knowing that other faithful servants of God had taken this path before Him, He was also sustained by the prophet's faith that come what may, the God who would vindicate Him was near, that God would give Him the courage to stay the course and the strength to see it through.

All of this is the deeper meaning, the inner script of the Palm Sunday drama, but it is a drama which is played out in our own daily lives as well. After all, it isn't just prophets and preachers who are criticized by others, who suffer slings and arrows or moments of doubt and despair. Everyone faces at one time or another the trials which test our spirits; we all are subject at some point in our lives to the tyranny of tears and fears.

I dare say we learn this early in life and never escape it.

I think first of teenagers, who live in that frustrating, confusing state called "adolescence." One day they feel all grown up; the next day they feel like children. One day they are wildly in love; the next day their broken hearts teach painful lessons about friendship and commitment, betrayal and disillusionment. One day they are saturated with sexual images in music, movies and advertising; the next day they are told they are too young to act on the sexual feelings growing within them. One day they are told that the future is theirs for the taking; the next day they see a world in chaos and wonder how kindly the future will treat them.

They want to know where the long arc of life is leading them, but, of course, no one can know what the future will bring. What they can know, however, is that faith makes the question much less terrifying than first it seems. In faith, they can know that the God who helps them is near, that no matter what may happen in the years ahead, God will be with them at every twist and turn in the road, helping them move onward to their destination in life. No, they cannot know what the future will bring, but they can know that God will be with them to see them through, and maybe that is all they really need to know.

Of course, we need that same faith in our adult years as well, with the problems of parenthood, the hard economic times and all the other pressures we face. But the longer I serve in ministry, the more I am convinced that this faith is most essential when we are very old, when we struggle through what we ruefully call our "golden years." I spend more time visiting with this group than any other in our church, and I cannot help but appreciate the tremendous courage and grace our older members possess.

Imagine taking your eyesight or your hearing for granted all of your life and then suddenly finding that it is failing you. Imagine being active and "on the go" for as long as you can remember, and then finding yourself virtually confined to your home. Imagine having legs so unsteady that a simple fall can be a catastrophe, or having bones so brittle that they break even as you sit in a chair! Imagine having to give up your home, along with all the furniture and accoutrements which have been part of your life for too many years to count. Imagine living long enough to watch all your brothers and sisters and your lifelong friends die one by one, until everyone who knew you in the prime of your life is gone! How many setbacks and losses is the human spirit to take before melancholy becomes one's permanent companion?

I visit people facing these and many other problems of aging, and I often find myself saying to them, "You know, you really are a very brave person." They invariably (and sincerely) protest that they are not brave at all, and I know what they are thinking. They are saying to themselves, "He doesn't know about the fears which flood my mind as I lie here alone at night. He doesn't know how lonely I feel, or how often I feel like giving up, or how the tears come to my eyes when we say the Lord's Prayer together — tears which come from places too deep to understand or explain. If he knew about things like that, he wouldn't think I am so very brave."

But I know something they don't know! You see, courage is not a matter of having no doubts or fears — courage is a matter of doing what you have to do in spite of your doubts and fears! Each day (and taking one day at a time), our older members do what they have to do in spite of whatever traumas or terrors may lurk without or within, and that is why I tell them I admire them for their courage.

During the long Cold War between nations on either side of the Iron Curtain, dissidents within the former Soviet Union struggled bravely for the cause of human rights against a communist state which observed few restraints in suppressing them. One of the most famous of such dissidents was Andrei Dmitrievich Sakharov (1921-1989), a prize-winning nuclear physicist and tireless gadfly on the body politic of the Soviet "people's republic."

As he neared the end of his life, Sakharov was increasingly determined to complete his memoirs, and not surprisingly, his totalitarian government was equally determined to see that those memoirs never saw the light of day. Eventually, the memoirs were smuggled out of the Soviet Union and published in the West, but the story of how hard it was to complete them is almost as interesting as the memoirs themselves.

Time and time again, Sakharov would write a section of his book, only to find that it had mysteriously vanished from its hiding place. Once, the half-written manuscript was stolen from a dentist's office; Sakharov gave his wife the news with trembling lips and a broken voice. Another time, when the project was nearly completed, it was stolen from a secret hiding place in the Sakharovs' car. Sakharov's wife said that when he discovered it was gone, he looked like he had just been told his best friend had died.

But each time, after pining a few days in discouragement, Sakharov would sit down and start writing again. Some parts were written better than before and others worse, but his wife explained how the book finally came to be: "My husband has a talent (I call it his main talent) to finish what he starts."[1]

On Palm Sunday, we look beyond the waving palms and triumphant parades to see Jesus facing His future and finding the courage to finish what He started. On Palm Sunday, we remember that Maundy Thursday and Good Friday lie between here and Easter Sunday. Forget the honor and praise we normally associate with this day, for honor can be a frivolous reward and praise is at best a fickle friend. Honeymoons end, bubbles burst, and friendly crowds shall disappear. Jesus shows us that what matters most is how we respond when the hour of testing draws near.

At every stage of life, there will be problems to dishearten and discourage us, but with faith they can never defeat us. There will be difficult situations which challenge us to the very limits of our endurance, but with faith they can never leave us crushed. With faith we can keep putting one foot in front of the other, because we know no valley is walked alone. "Behold, the Lord God helps me ... and I know I shall not be put to shame, [for] He who vindicates me is near."

Today our trials and troubles loom large before us, but at the end of our years, when all is said and done, we shall look back and say, "Yes, it was difficult at times, and I sometimes wondered how I would make it, but now I see I did not travel that hard road by myself. Now I see that no matter how arduous or overwhelming it seemed at the time, God was there to help me every step of the way. Now I can see that by His grace, I kept the faith and finished the race, and found within myself the strength to see it through." Amen.

---

1. Elena Bonner, *Alone Together* (translated by Alexander Cook, Knopf Publishers, New York).

Pastoral Prayer

Most Holy and Faithful God, who asks us not to let our heads be turned by public praises which come and go, but instead have our hearts set on You during moments both high and low, we gather with the cheering crowds this Palm Sunday morning as Your Son goes riding by. We call Him our King and hope we are faithful enough to put Him above every person or idea which would claim our highest loyalty. We call on Him to save us and pray we are willing to receive the salvation He offers. O God, we sing forth our easy praises today knowing that the greatest test is yet to come, for Your beloved Son and for all of us, Your children, as well.

Compassionate and Loving God, we pray we will pass as best we possibly can all the tests life may give us. Do not let us think we must face these tests alone, for this is surely an invitation to frustration and failure. Make us aware of Your nearness and help, that we may live with the confidence of knowing that the wounds which afflict us can never be fatal. Teach us, O God, to seek Your presence and pursue Your peace all the days of our lives, that filled with Your grace and guided by Your love, we may live faithfully in this world and gratefully in the next. In Jesus' name, we pray. Amen.

Children's Lesson
Palm Sunday/Passion Sunday
Text: Isaiah 50:4-9a

From Victim To Victor

"I gave my back to those who struck me ... I did not hide my face from insult and spitting." (Isaiah 50:6)

If you have brothers and sisters at home, you know that while life is always busy, life is not always pleasant. Yes. You know that brothers and sisters do mean things. Like taking the remote and not letting you have it. Like exiting your computer game before you saved it and you had gotten to the ninth level for the first time in your whole life. Like making themselves a sandwich for school lunch and not making you one. Like telling your parents when you do something bad and they do the same thing, too.

Well, what do most children do in situations like this? We all know the answer is obvious: they get even! You hide the remote so your brother or sister can't find it! You mess up their computer game on purpose. You make your own lunch and make sure not to make a lunch for anyone else. You find the first thing you can tattle about, and then you tell your parents what your sister or brother did, hoping to see them get punished ... the theory being that you will feel better when they feel worse.

Of course, these things *never* happen in my house, but I have *heard* they happen in other people's houses. Well, before we decide that getting even is the way to go, let's look at a man in the Bible named Isaiah, because he was someone who was always having mean things done to him. He was one of God's favorites, a prophet. God gave Isaiah messages He wanted Israel to hear, but most people didn't like what Isaiah had to say. Like telling them to be more fair to the poor. Like telling them to worship God with what they did in the world and not the words they say in church. Isaiah was brave and said things that made a lot of comfortable people feel very uncomfortable, and for this, he made lots of enemies.

So, people did mean things to him. They hit him. They made fun of him. They insulted him and even spit on him. Day after day, people tried to disgrace him in every way they could.

But Isaiah did not strike back. He did not say mean things back to people who said mean things to him. He did not spit on anyone or even complain to them. He simply let them be mean, and he trusted in God to keep him strong. "The Lord God helps me," he said, "and therefore I have not been disgraced."

People only disgrace you or insult you or hurt your feelings if you let them. People only make you mad if you let them. People only make you want to get even if you let yourself feel that way.

Try the other way sometimes. When someone (like a brother or sister, or someone at school) does something mean, let them! Let it go! Walk away! Say to yourself, "God helps me, so nothing this person is doing to me can hurt me." You won't feel like a victim who feels hurt and angry, you will feel like a victor — a winner — who feels strong and proud of yourself. You will feel like Isaiah, which means you will be glad, because God will feel very real to you, and you will know that God is helping you. Amen.

Sermon
Maundy Thursday
John 13:21-30

The Judas In Us All

"When Jesus had thus spoken, He was troubled in spirit, and testified, 'Truly, truly, I say to you, one of you will betray me.'" (John 13:21, RSV)

As we continue our journey to the agony of Calvary and the glory of Easter, certainly one of the major characters we meet along the way is Judas Iscariot, and surely one of the most intriguing questions of the Lenten season is, "Why did Judas do it?" Why did he make a deal with the authorities and turn Jesus over to His enemies? Why would someone betray the sinless Son of God?

I should begin by saying that Scripture gives no clear or simple answer to this question. All we can do is search the gospels for clues and offer our theories, for the motivations which lead the human heart to evil are multiple and complex.

Mark's gospel gives no reason for Judas' betrayal. Matthew suggests he did it for the money. Luke and John only say that Satan entered Judas' heart and led him to the authorities.

As for the theory that Judas did it for the money, Matthew has him saying to the priests, "What will you give me if I betray Jesus to you?" (26:15). And earlier, in John's gospel, we are told that Judas was a thief (12:6). He was the disciple in charge of the group's money, and John says Judas was stealing from the treasury.

To be perfectly honest with you, I don't buy it. It sounds like Matthew is trying to paint Judas as completely evil, without any redeeming qualities, and that could not have been the case. Remember that when Jesus said, "One of you will betray Me," the disciples all wondered who it might be. "Is it I, Lord? Is it I?" If Judas were utterly evil all along, the disciples would have known right away who the betrayer would be.

85

I suspect Luke and John are closer to the truth when they say that Satan entered Judas' heart. The devil made him do it. But I think the desire or inclination to do evil must have been building within Judas for a long time. After all, if Satan had just picked Judas out of the blue and forced him to betray Jesus, Judas would have been a mere pawn, a victim unlucky enough to be chosen for the deed (instead of John or Peter or Martha perhaps), without any real culpability or guilt.

No, when Satan enters a human heart and tempts that person to evil, the seeds of that evil have already been planted. Satan attacks the human heart at the point where it is most predisposed to sin, but that predisposition must already be there.

Assuming, then, that Judas didn't do it for the money, what was the gathering weakness within that led him to betray Jesus? What finally allowed Satan to lead Judas to the authorities? Here we find a huge clue by looking at the people to whom Judas went to strike his bargain of betrayal — the chief priests.

The chief priests wanted Jesus dead, and they were very clear about why. They feared Rome. More particularly, they feared what Rome would do to Israel because of Jesus. Jesus had become too popular, too powerful. Too many Israelites — subjects of the Roman Empire — were calling Jesus "Messiah" and "King."

It is all spelled out in the eleventh chapter of John, when the chief priests say to one another, "If we let [Jesus] go on like this, everyone will believe in him, and the Romans will come and destroy both our holy place and our nation." Then Caiaphas, the high priest, says to them, "You know nothing at all! You do not understand that it is better for you to have one man die for the people than to have the whole nation destroyed" (vv. 47-50).

So, Judas might well have thought he was saving Israel by betraying Jesus. As the tension mounted between Jesus, the Jewish authorities, and Rome, Judas may simply have lost his nerve and lacked the strength to see it through. "Jesus has gotten too big; He has gone too far," Judas may have said to himself. "Why, just the other day He started a riot in the Temple, antagonizing the money-changers and the priests. We must be practical about such things.

This talk about Messiahs and new kingdoms is foolish and dangerous ... We must consider the possible consequences. For the good of the nation, I must betray Him."

For whatever reason, the desire to betray Jesus was building within Judas. Finally, the crescendo became a climax at the Last Supper, when Jesus announced His betrayal was at hand. Immediately confusion, loud denials, and plaintive questions erupted as the disciples tried to determine who would commit such an evil act.

Jesus' spirit was surely troubled as He considered what Judas was about to do. To be betrayed is bad enough, but to be betrayed by someone in whom you had once placed your confidence and trust is much crueler. Jesus may have thought back to the day Judas first answered His call. He may have thought back to the day when Judas' faith in Him was young and pure — back to the early days, before the crowds and the miracles, before the politics and the high priests — when Judas had walked and talked with Him for hours about the law and the prophets, faith and salvation.

Now, by flickering candlelight in the Upper Room, Jesus saw a different Judas, an older Judas, a Judas who no longer believed in Him as he once did. He saw the pain in Judas' eyes as he rose to leave, as Judas turned his back on the Light of the world and walked out into the darkness. John's gospel says simply, "Judas immediately went out, and it was night" (13:30).

If we grieve tonight for what the world did to Jesus, grieve also for poor Judas. Once his name was an honorable one, meaning "worthy to be praised." Now the name of Judas is an oath, an obscenity, and so it will always remain. In the rock opera *Jesus Christ Superstar,* Judas screams out in despair, "Just don't say I am damned for all time!" But that is precisely what Judas is: damned for all time.

But grieve also for ourselves and our world, for the truth is, there is a piece of Judas in all of us. This is the real horror of what Judas did, regardless of why you think he did it, and this is the real meaning we should find in Judas on this Maundy Thursday night. Let no one be smug and say we would not have done what Judas did, for tonight we see that there is a Judas within us all.

If he did it for the money, does that not happen all the time today? How many people do things in their lives they know Christ would not have them do, because it pays well?

Jesus said, "You cannot serve God and wealth" (Luke 16:13), but how often have all of us, at every level of society, cut ethical corners at home or on the job and betrayed the witness of Jesus Christ because the money is good? How often have we turned Christ's words upside down to justify our own privilege and profit? How many times have people said in their own way what Judas said so long ago: "What will you give me if I betray Jesus to you?"

Even more disturbing is the other possible reason for Judas' betrayal. Like him, we turn Jesus over to His enemies every time we say, "Jesus has gone too far. His way is foolish and dangerous. We must be practical and think of the consequences; we can't let this religious thing get out of hand. All this talk about putting God above nation, race, and even family, this 'bleeding heart' talk about caring for the poor, turning the other cheek, and loving our enemies — this is worse than naive! I suppose this Jesus thing is all right up to a point, but we shouldn't get carried away with it!"

Every time we say Jesus goes too far — every time we turn from His ways because we think they are foolish and impractical — we become like Judas. Judas had his reasons and he thought they were good ones, and so do we. But Judas betrayed his Lord.

Where is your weakest point, which Satan might use to turn you against your Savior? Are you finding reasons to say that Jesus' way is unrealistic, that it goes too far, that He couldn't have really meant what He said and His words must be watered down to be at all sensible in this world? Are you starting to fit Jesus into your ways instead of fitting yourself into His?

In the spirit of Lamentations: "Let us test and examine our ways, and return to the Lord" (3:40). In the warning of Jeremiah: "I the Lord test the mind and search the heart, to give to all according to their ways, according to the fruit of their doings" (17:10). There is a Judas within us all. Find it out and stop it, before it leads you to the high priests.

On this Maundy Thursday night, as we share the Lord's Supper, Jesus is saying again, "The one who betrays Me is eating bread with Me." Amen.

Sermon
Easter Sunday
Texts: Jeremiah 31:31-34; Luke 24:36-49

Resurrection Of The Heart

"I will put My law within them, and I will write it on their hearts."
(Jeremiah 31:33b)

I demand that you love me!
That's right — I insist that every one of you love me and be courteous and fair to me at all times. In fact, I recommend that we amend our church's bylaws to read: "All members of this church shall be required to love the minister unconditionally."

But wait: that doesn't go far enough. I also demand that you love one another. I order you to be good to each other and treat each other respectfully in every way possible, and to ensure that you do this, I think we should write a bylaw which mandates each of you to feel nothing but love for everyone else in the church.

But why stop with our church? See how mean-spirited our nation has become, how people are divided against one another by age and race and region; see how the poor are being systematically abandoned because we think we can no longer afford to care about their plight? I think we should go to Washington and get a law passed which requires all Americans to love each other and decrees that all future laws written by our legislators must be guided by the principles of compassion and concern.

Come to think of it: the world could use such a law as well! We have nations waging cruel wars against other nations; we have bloody ethnic and tribal conflicts within nations; we have millions of innocent children starving every day in a world which has enough food for everyone. Let's go to the United Nations and pass a resolution which requires people everywhere to stop all this at once! We need a law throughout the world which *compels* people to treat each other as they would want others to treat them.

It doesn't work that way, does it? Law can regulate behavior, but it cannot compel feelings or affections. When I tell my three children they cannot watch their Saturday morning cartoons until they have put away all their toys, I am not transforming them into conscientious little creatures who suddenly want to be clean and responsible for their things. My Saturday morning edicts can only make them *go through the motions* of being clean and responsible for their things ... and under duress and protest, at that! In their heart of hearts, they still want to treat our entire house as the world's largest playpen, and no rules or regulations from me will change that innate desire any time soon.

God had the same problem with His children, that is to say, with us. He made a covenant with us and gave us His law to live by because He wanted us to enjoy the fullness and abundance of life. Life as God created it is "very good" (Genesis 1:31), and the idea behind our obeying God's law is that we only know how good life really can be when we live by His will instead of our own.

There were the Ten Commandments, of course (and most of us could probably recite at least six of them by heart!), but God's law was much more than a set of "do's" and "don'ts" for personal living. There was also an attitude, an inner disposition, a direction in life which the law sought to instill in us. "You shall love the Lord your God with all your heart, and with all your soul and with all your might." This is the *Shema*, the heart of God's law. "Recite [these words] to your children," the Scripture says, "and talk about them ... Write them on the doorposts of your house and on your gates." Live by this law at all times, God said, and "it shall go well for you" (cf. Deuteronomy 6:1-9).

But the law was not enough to make it "go well for us" as God's people. As my children demonstrate every Saturday morning and as the world has demonstrated throughout the tragedy which is human history, the desire to do right and walk in God's path cannot be compelled by outside threat or edict. It has to come from within.

Clearly, we needed a new way to live with God, a new way of enjoying a relationship with God, and God finally announced through His prophet Jeremiah that He would give us that way. "Behold, the days are coming," said God, "when I will make a new covenant with [My people]." It won't be like the old covenant, in which God's law was written on tablets of stone and given to us to obey. This time, that same law (which is still good and true) shall be written on our hearts. This time, we shall instinctively know God's will for our lives and shall instinctively be able to do it.

Sometimes, of course, we do live God's law of love instinctively. Sometimes it is as natural to us as breathing, and we don't even think about it. For example, when a mother must send her young child to school in the pouring rain, she puts on his raincoat and ties the hood on his head to keep him dry. Does she do this because she is afraid if she doesn't — if she lets him go out in the rain without a coat and hat — she might be charged with child neglect? She doesn't even think in legal terms like that; she dresses him for the nasty weather simply because she loves her child!

There are many other situations in our daily lives where we give ourselves to others, not because we must but because we may. We wish we could be that way all the time, but, of course, we are not — not with nearby loved ones and certainly not with distant strangers whose names we do not know and whose needs we do not heed. Deep in our hearts, we want to be the love and compassion of God in every way we can, but something inside holds us back. We want to be the kindness and generosity we admire so much in Jesus, but something inside puts limits on the amount of kindness we give.

Perhaps we are simply too needy ourselves to be gentle with the needs of others. The quick temper, the unhappy compulsion, the brooding pessimism which protects against disappointment — what are these but reactions to the pains and heartaches we ourselves have suffered over the years? The poisonous tongue which continually spreads a discouraging word — what is this but a symptom of our own discouragement, a symptom of the inner hurts which drive us on to hurt?

What do we desire more fervently than to live in communion with God, and what do we mourn more deeply than our separation from God? There is in every human heart a reservoir of spiritual injury and pain which only God's presence can heal. There is in every human heart an emptiness, a desolation, a yearning for connection which only God's presence can answer. Try as we might to do God's will, there remains within us a restlessness, a spiritual hunger, which only God's presence — and not merely His law — can satisfy.

Today on Easter Sunday, as God promised so long ago through Jeremiah, the connection is made and the empty spaces are filled. Today, the inner wounds are healed and we can finally be the love we have always longed to be. Easter means that the kingdom of God is no longer some distant ideal we strive grimly to reach but never grasp; now "the kingdom of God is within you" (Luke 17:21) and me and every other child of God, because today, God has given us a new covenant, written not on two tablets of stone but in the temple of every human heart. Today, our sad and solitary struggles for happiness are over, and we are united at last with our joy.

Of course, this inner healing and transformation doesn't happen just because we say so, or because Jesus Christ was raised from the grave two thousand years ago in Jerusalem. As much as God wants this new covenant for us, we still must do something to receive it, and it is not as simple as it sounds. In a word, we must accept something which appears in both of our texts and speaks to the very essence of the meaning of Christ's Resurrection.

In our text from Luke, Jesus explains that He had to "suffer and rise from the dead on the third day" in order that "repentance and forgiveness of sins [can be] proclaimed in His name to all nations." And in our text from Jeremiah, God announces the key to His new covenant by saying, "I will forgive their iniquity and remember their sin no more."

Forgiveness! If there is one theme which runs throughout the whole history of creation, it is God's consistent effort to offer us forgiveness. We disobey God's verbal instructions in the Garden of Eden, but God does not give up on us; He sends us written commandments to live by. We disregard the written commandments, but God does not give up on us; He sends His prophets to call us back to His covenant law. We persecute the prophets God sends, but God *still* doesn't give up on us; He sends His only begotten Son to save us. Then we crucify God's Son and, even now, God does not despise or give up on us. Instead, God raises His Son from the dead, once again repaying our rebelliousness with forgiveness and, this time, adding the gift of eternal life as well.

That is the whole history of the Bible in twenty seconds! But we should also know that this larger history of creation is replicated in microcosm in the history of our own individual lives. We each in our own ways have continually turned away from the lives God asks us to live, but God has revealed Himself throughout history and throughout our lives as wanting nothing but to forgive us. Indeed, the ultimate sign of God's forgiveness is here at the empty tomb, and still our hearts are burdened! How much happier we would be if we would simply accept the pardon God is so eager to give us!

A pastor received a letter from a parishioner at a former church, catching him up on the past year's news:

> *What a year! We married my brother George last fall. We had our baby, John, Jr. Aunt Ida died and my father-in-law is dying in a nursing home. With the school referendum and the natural joys and sorrows of four children, I feel as if we are on a perpetual emotional jag. Our next door neighbor kicked her teenage daughter out of the house and told her not to come back. Another neighbor and mother of four had a nervous breakdown. And the friendly couple down the street have become alcoholics. What we need in this town is someone to come along and show us the meaning of this crazy life and to preach "forgiveness, forgiveness, forgiveness!" Isn't it strange how everything seems to boil down either to our being unable to forgive others, or feeling guilty and unforgiven ourselves?*

Today on Easter Sunday, can we at last believe what God has been telling us all along — that He loves and forgives us still? Can we believe that the tangled knots into which we tie our tortured lives are cut clean today with the single stroke of God's amazing grace, that the melancholy weight we carry within is lifted from our aching hearts at last? Can we believe on this Easter morning that in spite of everything we know about ourselves, in spite of all the ways we have betrayed our faith and held back our love from God, that we are finally and fully forgiven today?

Of course, some people forgive without really forgiving. A certain man was once compelled to ask his wife, "Why do you keep talking about all my past mistakes? I thought you had agreed to forgive and forget?" "I have, indeed, forgiven and forgotten," his wife replied. "But I want to make sure *you* don't forget that I have forgiven and forgotten!"

God's forgiveness is not like that. God says, "I will forgive your iniquity and remember your sins no more." Remember our sins no more! They are gone — forgotten — forgiven and forgotten! A new covenant written in the penmanship of love has healed our wounded hearts and mended our broken spirits, filling in the empty places inside and answering the deepest longings of our souls. Can we believe it?

In other years, we might speak of the many other meanings of Easter. One year, we might speak about the death of death and the gift of eternal life. In another year, we might speak about the world's suffering and injustice, the sorrow and the pity around us, and how Christ's resurrection promises that the future belongs not to the powers of darkness but to the Power of God's light. I suppose we could hear Easter sermons for decades to come and never exhaust the full meaning of this glorious day.

But this year, let Easter be for us the ultimate sign of God's forgiveness. This year, let Easter's resurrection take place within our hearts, that we may finally accept the pardon God is trying so hard to give us, that we may lay down our weary burdens and start living the rest of our lives in freedom, faith and grace.

Can we believe we are forgiven today? Can we let our hearts soar and our lives be changed now that the slate of our soul's offenses has been wiped clean by the unending mercy of God?

Let me be more specific: can each of *you* truly believe in the secret places of your heart that you are forgiven today? So much depends on it, and an empty tomb says you can. Amen.

Pastoral Prayer

Most Gracious and Powerful God, whose love for us is stronger than death and whose mercy extends beyond the grave, we come to the empty tomb today as the first disciples came so long ago ... struggling to believe the incredible sight our eyes have seen. Because of the empty tomb, we who have tried off and on with varying degrees of effort to live by Your law have now had the slate of our shortcomings wiped clean, but we know ourselves so well that we have trouble believing You could really forgive us.

Help us, O Lord, to believe the good news of this Easter morning. Help us to believe that at last we are forgiven by a God whose grace is beyond measure. Help us to accept the pardon You have offered and make us free at last, that we may live in the new covenant You have labored so hard to give us. O God, make us believers in Your tender mercy today, that the desire to do Your will in the world shall flow as naturally from our hearts as Your love has flowed to us.

Finally, O God, we pray for resurrection not only in our hearts but throughout the world as well. We pray for a new way in the world, a new covenant of love and nonviolence, of justice, mercy and peace. We pray today believing that such a world will come, for we are people who have seen the future, and the future is an empty tomb. In Jesus' name. Amen.

Children's Lesson
Easter Sunday
Text: Luke 24:36-49

Ghost Stories

"They were startled and terrified, and thought that they were seeing a ghost." (Luke 24:37)

How many of you have ever seen a ghost? *(Let them answer.)* Have you ever seen ghosts in the movies? What do they look like in the movies? Do you think ghosts are real?

How many of you have ever heard or read a ghost story? *(Let them answer.)* Boy, I remember one I heard as a child ... it was an old story called "The Telltale Heart," and it was told to a group of us at night in an old dark barn with just a single lantern in the barn. The man who told it to us could really tell a story. I mean, he could do the scary voices and the sound effects and everything! How do you think I felt? That's right, I was scared silly! I was sitting really close to the children next to me. That's how we feel when we read ghost stories, or see movies with ghosts in them, isn't it? Ghosts are supposed to make us scared.

Well, I don't think ghosts are real, and I have never seen one, except in the movies, and we KNOW movies aren't real, right? But the Bible tells us that a group of Jesus' friends *thought* they saw a ghost, and it scared them, too! It happened on Easter Sunday.

Sometimes we forget that the first Easter was scary. Today we make Easter full of fresh flowers and brand-new clothes and beautiful music and happy people, but remember: Jesus' friends on that first Easter were scared. In fact, the Bible says they were terrified. Some had seen Jesus die — they had seen Him die with their own eyes! And now that they thought they were seeing Him alive again, they thought they were really seeing a ghost.

Of course, the reason we celebrate Easter as such a happy day is that it wasn't a ghost they saw. It was really Jesus, alive again after being dead and buried for three days. His friends saw Him and spoke with Him and touched Him and ate with Him. They saw, not a ghost at all, but the Risen Son of God.

They saw the Man who had died for all of our sins, and the Man who then showed that after we die, we rise up and live again. He proved it to us, and so the thing we fear the most is now nothing to be feared. That's why Easter is so glorious and happy and wondrous and beautiful. That is why all of you look so beautiful today.

It's odd, isn't it? We go to a movie to see make-believe ghosts pretending to be real ghosts, and we get scared. But on Easter, Jesus' friends thought they saw a *real* ghost which turned out *not* to be a ghost, and suddenly they had no reason to be frightened any more. Amen.

Sermon
Sunday After Easter
Text: John 20:19-31

Late For Easter

"But Thomas, one of the twelve, was not with them when Jesus came."
(John 20:24)

There have been a number of occasions in my life where I have had the opportunity to make a complete fool of myself, and sad to say, I have generally taken full advantage of each one of those opportunities as they came along. I suppose I could prove the point by regaling you with dozens of pertinent stories, but for the sake of preserving your time and my dignity, I will tell you just one.

The incident took place in my early twenties when I was spending part of a winter in Paris. It was a case of my having enough money to get to Paris but not enough to live on once I got there; I was living in the artists' quarter on the Left Bank in a one-room flat with no heat or hot water. The bathroom was three floors below me and the shower consisted of a plain garden hose and a wash bucket to stand in. I thought I would get a good dose of the romantic, bohemian lifestyle in Paris that winter. In fact, all I got was the worst cold I have ever suffered in my life.

One night, I decided to go the Opera House. It wasn't that I liked opera or had even heard one before, but it was something I thought I should do while I was in Paris.

I arrived just as the large crowd was filing inside to find their seats, and right away I had a problem — another man was sitting in the seat I had paid for. The performance was starting, and even though I showed the intruder my ticket for that seat, he kept asking me where I had been and refused to move. The people behind us were protesting, but I persisted, and when the man finally got up to leave, he muttered something about "stupid Americans" as he headed angrily up the aisle.

"How rude," I thought as I settled down to watch the opera. However, the upset I felt was quickly forgotten as the soaring music of Puccini's *La Boheme* filled the hall. Like I said, my own musical tastes had never tilted towards opera, but I have always appreciated good melodies and harmonies, and Puccini was a master at both. I fell in love with the music I heard that night, and to this day, even though it is the only opera I have ever listened to, I have four different renditions of *La Boheme* at home.

Although I couldn't really understand the lyrics that night, I began to get a rough idea of what was going on. But then, quite suddenly it seemed, the heroine died, the audience applauded, the house lights came back on and people began to leave. I thought it was rather strange that poor Mimi had died so early in the opera, but as I followed the crowd out to the lobby, I figured I would come back for the second half and see how the story ended.

That's when I realized what had happened. The audience was going home because the opera was over! I had misread the starting time on my ticket and arrived during the intermission, thinking the opera was just beginning. No wonder the man in my seat asked me where I had been and thought I was dense! I had come in late, but because I didn't know the first thing about *La Boheme* or any other opera, it never dawned on me that I had missed the whole first half of the performance! I was glad no one in the Paris audience knew me that night, because I felt rather ignorant and foolish.

Of course, I am not the only person ever to feel foolish like that, and I know I am not the only person ever to be late for something, either. On any given day, children are late for school and parents are late for work. People are late for everything from doctors' appointments to graduation ceremonies, and occasionally they are even late for church! I once officiated at a wedding where the bride was three hours late for no apparent reason, and I was also involved in a funeral where we had to sit around waiting for the casket to arrive! The next time you scold some "slowpoke" by saying, "Why, you'll even be late for your own funeral," don't think it couldn't happen!

But the all-time, most significant example of being late and looking foolish is found in our text and belongs to a much-maligned disciple named Thomas. That's right, the man we have always called "Doubting Thomas" can also be called "Tardy Thomas," because our text says Thomas was not with the other disciples when the Resurrected Jesus appeared. Thomas was late for Easter.

We can only speculate as to where Thomas was when the other disciples were gathered behind locked doors. Maybe, after hearing about Jesus' trial and execution, Thomas had gone off somewhere seeking solitude in his grief. A long ride in the country, a few easy-to-read drugstore novels to get his mind off things, and most of all, some time alone would be good for his soul.

Maybe Thomas had gone home to catch up on some chores he had let slide over the last three years. The wife had asked that he fix the back screen door, and the roof had needed new shingles for a long time, but Thomas had been off roaming the countryside with Jesus. Maybe Thomas felt it was time to go home and take care of some domestic responsibilities which had been too long neglected.

Or maybe Thomas had simply decided to reevaluate the direction of his life. A few years earlier, he had thought about joining the Peace Corps, but then Jesus came along and Thomas had become a disciple instead. But now, perhaps it was time to end this youthful "social action fling" and go back to medical school, settle down and get on with a more conventional life.

Whatever reason Thomas may have had for not being present when Christ appeared to the other disciples, the bottom line is that Thomas was late for Easter. He did not miss the beginning of the story as I had done in Paris, but Thomas did miss a critical part of a continuing story, and he was all the poorer for it.

Because he was late for Easter, Thomas had his doubts about the Resurrection. The other disciples had searched him out and found him, telling him in excited tones that they had seen the Risen Savior, but Thomas had responded with disbelief. "I can't buy that," he replied. "Unless I see Him myself, see His wounded hands and touch His wounded side, I will not change my mind."

Because Thomas was late for Easter, he had his doubts about the Resurrection, and because he had his doubts about the Resurrection, Thomas was not empowered. He was still the same disillusioned, terrified, and confused man he had been on Good Friday, while the other disciples were now transformed. Once forlorn and even cowardly themselves, now they were filled with power and grace (Acts 4:33) because they had experienced Easter Sunday. The same Lord who just last week seemed dead and defeated was now alive again, and they had seen this with their own eyes!

What else could possibly matter more to them than this staggering new reality? How else could they feel but strengthened and emboldened and eager to tell the world this astounding good news, even at the cost of their lives? The other disciples were new people imbued with a revolutionary new power and Spirit — only Thomas remained as he had been before.

"As the Father has sent Me, so I send you." The rest of the disciples were ready to be sent as Christ was sent ... sent to suffer and serve, sent as people transformed to transform the world and turn it "upside down" (Acts 17:6). Peter would end up in Rome and Andrew in what is now Russia. James would go to Syria while Matthew would go to Persia and Ethiopia. Others would be sent to the veritable four corners of the earth to continue the story of Easter. Only Thomas remained ... unenlightened, unchanged, uninspired, with nowhere to go and no story to tell.

The disciples met a week after Easter, just as we are meeting here today, and this time, Thomas was persuaded to join them. Suddenly Jesus appeared in their midst, and Thomas' eyes told his heart what to believe. "My Lord and my God!" he cried. It may have come a week late, but now Easter was as real to Thomas as it had been to the others. Truly, it is better to come to Easter late than never to arrive there at all.

"As the Father has sent Me, so I send you." Regardless of when you or I "see" the Risen Christ through the eyes of faith — whether the reality of Easter takes hold of us early in the morning or late in the day — Jesus' words change our lives the moment we come to that faith. Indeed, once we believe with all our heart, soul and mind that Christ the Lord is risen from the grave, how can it be any other way? Like Mary and Thomas and countless other saints before us, we are sent into the world by Christ as Christ Himself was sent to the world by God.

"As the Father sent Me, so do I send you" to live out your resurrection faith in your homes and families. Be the moral and spiritual guide your children will need, that they may receive a foundation to uphold them the rest of their lives. Be the sensitive spirit and listening ear your parents will need as they abide the shifting fortunes of age. By the power of the resurrection you now have witnessed and hold within you, make your families academies of deeper humanity, where young and old alike may learn to give love unconditionally and receive it in the way it is given.

"As the Father sent Me, so do I send you" to live out your resurrection faith in your places of work. Be the exemplar of integrity in your office, store, or factory, going the extra mile to understand and serve the needs of others. Be a conscience in your company, that fairness may be the product and compassion the process as you labor with others under the sun. By the power of the resurrection you now have witnessed and hold within you, make your workplaces engines of equity and social responsibility, where doing good is at least as important as doing well.

"As the Father sent Me, so do I send you" to live out your resurrection faith in your church. Be the embodiment of Christian charity in all your church dealings, seeking to build up and bind together rather than tear down and rip apart. Be a model of kindness in thought, word, and deed, that kindness might flourish in all God's people. By the power of the resurrection you now have witnessed and hold within you, make your church a community of repentance and forgiveness, that it may be leaven for the world and nourishment for the soul as God intends it to be.

Finally, "as the Father sent Me, so do I send you" to live out your resurrection faith in the troubled world around you. Be an ambassador of God's love to all people near and far, friend and foe, that others may seek for themselves the divine light they see shining in you. Be architects of justice and builders of righteousness, hoping against hope that the will of God shall someday bless the earth. By the power of the resurrection you now have witnessed and hold within you, help make the world a gentler place for those who suffer its various cruelties, that God might someday be more pleased with our use of His creation.

All of this and more is the call Christ gave last Easter Sunday to modern-day disciples like us who gather in His name. But sometimes we don't hear that call when it is first given because something is blocking our ears and blinding our hearts. Something inside is making us late for Easter. Circumstances arise and events intervene to oppress our spirits, leaving us inwardly unprepared to see and believe the Risen Lord who stands before us. Sometimes, like Thomas, we don't get the good news of Easter on the day God chooses to give it.

Perhaps that is true for some of us this year. If, a week after the Resurrection, some of us feel uninspired and unempowered as Thomas felt so long ago, know that Christ is visiting us still to show us His wounds and share His victory. Know that He comes again and again to tell us the good news, and when we finally hear it — when our eyes behold at last the Risen Christ and our hearts believe what our eyes have seen — then we are transformed from within by power and grace abounding, ready to conquer all that troubles us and ready to be sent forth in service to others as Christ was sent forth in service to us.

Trumpets are playing and triumph's song is sounding in these days which follow Easter. My Lord and my God, we hear them at last! My Lord and my God, we see You risen and believe at last! The time is upon us and we dare not be late, for Christ calls us even as I speak to live with new faith, hope, and love in the wondrous new world His death and resurrection have made. Amen.

Pastoral Prayer

O Good and Gracious God, whose plan for our salvation was written before the world was made and who asks us to continue that plan in the way we live our lives, we come to You today acknowledging that some of us were late for Easter this year. We didn't get the good news as it was read and preached and sung last week, or we felt it for a moment but lost it once we left Your house. We were too absorbed with other things, or crises arose to distract us, and now we lack the inspiration we think we should have at this time of year because we missed seeing the Risen Christ appear in our midst.

But You, O God, have sent a Savior who is patient and merciful with us. He comes now to visit those of us who missed seeing Him before, that our joy may be no less complete than those who saw Him first. He shows us His wounds that we may not fear to endure our own, and He sends us out to serve as He Himself was sent to serve.

O God, do not let us be late in answering that call. Do not let the problems which grip us make us blind to the promise You have placed within our grasp. Even today, on this Sunday after Easter, help us receive the good news of our Risen Lord, for we need it in the very depths of our souls, and we would rather receive it late than never receive it at all. In Jesus' name, we pray. Amen.

Children's Lesson
Sunday After Easter
Text: John 20:19-31

Be A Doubting Thomas

"But he [Thomas] said to them, 'Unless I see the mark of the nails in His hands ... I will not believe.' " (John 20:25)

Last week we talked about ghosts and how hard it was for even Jesus' best friends to believe that He was alive again after He was dead. Well, by this time — a week after Easter — most of Jesus' close friends had seen Him alive and believed it. But there was one man named Thomas who still did not believe.

Some people came rushing to him and said, "Thomas! Thomas! Come quickly! Jesus is alive!" But Thomas had his doubts. Thomas was one of those guys who has to see something with his own eyes before he can believe it. Thomas was one of those guys who, if someone were to say, "I can jump all the way across this sidewalk without touching it," he would say, "Oh, yeah? Let's see you do it." Thomas was one of those guys who, if someone were to say, "I'll give you one hundred dollars for that bicycle," he would say, "Oh, yeah? Show me the money!"

Thomas was not a man easily fooled. When people came to him and said Jesus was alive, Thomas said, in effect, "Oh, yeah? Show me. I won't believe it until I can touch the places where the nails wounded His hands. Then I can see and believe for myself."

Ever since then, he has been called Doubting Thomas. And ever since then, people in church have used Doubting Thomas as an example of what *not* to be. "Don't be a doubting Thomas!" they say, to children and adults alike. When it comes to believing in God and Jesus and Christmas and Easter and all the things we talk about here in church, some people say we shouldn't have doubts. We must have faith.

Is it okay for your minister to tell you that? I'm not so sure. Sometimes doubting is a good thing. And sometimes the best way to believe in something is first to have doubts about it.

Suppose I were to tell you, "I believe that if you ran as fast as you can towards that wall over there, and if you wish really hard and don't stop running, you can run right through that wall like magic and not be hurt." Are you going to believe that? Are you going to try it? No! Not a chance! Not unless you want to make a mess of your face! You're going to have doubts about it, and those doubts will keep you from getting hurt. That's a case of it being good to doubt, isn't it?

Sometimes doubting can help you believe. Suppose I told you that if you took two balls of the same size and shape up to the top of a very tall building — one ball weighs ten pounds and the other weighs one pound — and you dropped them both at the same time, they would hit the ground at the exact same moment. "No way," you say. "I don't believe it. The heavier ball falls faster because it weighs more. It has to fall faster!"

You have your doubts, so you try it. And the two balls hit the ground together. You still have your doubts, so you take two other balls, one light and one heavy, and you try it again. The same thing happens: they hit the ground at the same time. You try it five or six more times, and finally you believe that heavy and light objects of the same size and shape fall to the ground at the same speed. Now you believe it would happen the same way every time and everywhere you tried it, and no one can make you stop believing it.

Well, that is a case of doubts helping you to believe something. So you see, it's nice to have faith and believe, but it can also be okay to have your doubts, because doubts can be the seeds of a very strong faith. That is what happened with Thomas. He had his doubt about Jesus being raised from the dead, so he went to see for himself. And once he did, he believed and never doubted his faith again. Amen.

www.ingramcontent.com/pod-product-compliance
Lightning Source LLC
Chambersburg PA
CBHW071721040426
42446CB00011B/2169